The Customer
Is Always Wrong

The Customer Is Always Wrong

The Retail Chronicles

Edited and Compiled by Jeff Martin

SOFT SKULL PRESS

BROOKLYN

Library of Congress Cataloging-in-Publication Data

The customer is always wrong : the retail chronicles / edited
by Jeff Martin.
    p. cm.
 1. Sales personnel--Humor. 2. Selling--Humor. I. Martin,
Jeff, 1980- II. Title.

 PN6231.S17C87 2008
 658.8'120207--dc22

                      2008014082

ISBN (10): 1-933368-90-X
ISBN (13): 978-1-93336-890-0

Cover and interior design by David Janik
Printed in the United States of America

Soft Skull Press
An Imprint of Counterpoint LLC
2117 Fourth Street
Suite D
Berkeley, CA 94710

www.softskull.com
www.counterpointpress.com

Distributed by Publishers Group West

10 9 8 7 6 5 4 3 2 1

What the customer demands is last year's model, cheaper. To find out what the customer needs you have to understand what the customer is doing as well as he understands it. Then you build what he needs and you educate him to the fact that he needs it.

—Edna St. Vincent Millay

I'd just like to be treated like a regular customer.

—Elvis Presley

Contents

Foreword
Neal Pollack

Once upon a time, billions of retail transactions ago, my family took a weekend trip to the Grand Canyon. We stayed at the Bright Angel Lodge, as it afforded maximum views with minimum walking. One afternoon, we went to the restaurant for lunch. We ordered our food. It didn't come. We asked after the order. Still, it didn't come. Eventually, my father complained to the manager. Our order wasn't coming, the manager said, because we'd been "rude to the waitress." Well, this sent my father into apoplexy. Lawsuits were threatened and lunch was demanded that instant. In the family-legend retelling of the story, four hours later, another waitress finally arrived, took our order again, and we got our precious lunch.

Nearly thirty years later, all the family participants in that event are still alive, and the "rude to the waitress" comment still gets trotted out in the face of bad service, or even the anticipation of bad service. Enough, I want to say. Please stop bringing up that unpleasant day.

That incident truly traumatized me. Since then, I've been on either end of a retail transaction countless times, and I often still wonder about the Grand Canyon restaurant debacle. What if we *had* been rude to the waitress? What if the lack of service had been something we'd deserved? It's not as though we're incapable. I've seen my father send back an egg twice because it wasn't poached to his liking. I've certainly seen my mom get bitchy at the bank. And I'm hardly a saint in the retail environment. For every ten pleasant exchanges of goods and services, there's one where I huff and shuffle my feet restlessly, and, very occasionally, one where I storm out in furious indignation.

Then again, my dad is the only person I know who has a personal relationship with the butcher in his neighborhood chain grocery store. He's a welcome fixture at a central Phoenix black-owned BBQ restaurant. Sometimes, he can be a great customer. So can I. So can we all.

Every day, we step into an impossible dance of commercial interactions with completely anonymous strangers. Sometimes we comport ourselves well, sometimes poorly, and it doesn't matter. Yes, there are rules of etiquette and basic human decency, but who cares if you get tossed out of a Jamba Juice when there's another Jamba Juice a mile down the road? Is Larry David a hero for calling out his dry cleaner's hypocritical service policy, is he an idiot, or is he both?

The essays in this collection do nothing to soothe my mind, calm my neuroses, or answer my questions. But they do show me that I'm not alone in my confusion. We'll all be waiters and waited upon, respected, disrespected, and ignored, every day for the rest of our lives until the planet finally implodes and we don't have to worry about being customers any more. I, for one, look forward to that time.

Introduction
Jeff Martin

I would like to tell you that my entire retail career has been one long social experiment intended to get to the heart of what makes working America tick. But if I told you that, I would be lying. I'm no Barbara Ehrenreich. Nor do I wish to be. That poor woman has seen and experienced things that would push me to the brink of psychosis. One shift working in your average department store would most certainly transform me into some kind of retail vigilante, beating members of upper management with the baseball bats found on the sporting goods aisle.

In all honesty, my retail life has been, for the most part, free of excessive humiliation and degradation (note the word *excessive*). But there are common threads that run throughout the industry. No matter what product you're selling or where you happen to live, there is one aspect of retail that is the same the world over: assholes. And it's not just the customers and passers-by. It's everybody. It's co-workers, bosses, parcel carriers, garbage collectors, janitors, and every other group you can think of. The only difference between a customer who is an asshole and just your regular asshole off the street is this: You don't have to be nice to a regular asshole. If your paperboy gives you the finger as he delivers the evening edition, you can freely give it back to him without fear of disciplinary action or termination.

This is not the case in a retail environment.

The purpose of this book, if any, is to show the light at the end of the tunnel. These writers are retail survivors. They made it to the other side of the river with their sanity intact. The Employee Identification Number tattooed on their forearms is a painful reminder of the past and a source of motivation for the future.

Retail seems to be the most transitory job in the world, even to those who've been doing it for years. I have never met or worked with someone who said, "I'm here. I made it." Quite the opposite in fact. You can't work a week in retail without hearing about someone's dreams and aspirations, farfetched though some may be. I don't know about you, but I find something hopeful in that. You never hear doctors saying, "Well this medicine stuff is just a way to pay the bills until I find my true calling." No, retail people are searchers, the nomads of the American workforce.

If this book can help shed a little more light on the often-disregarded retail experience, then we have done our job and done it well. And if you, Dear Reader, just so happen to be one of the assholes I mentioned earlier (and you know if you are), just try to go easy on your local customer service representatives. They are just trying to do their jobs.

And no, you can't return that without a receipt.

Sears, Sbarro's, Sayonara
Wade Rouse

"I am Sssshhhearssshh!"

Day one in retail.

Day one as an official adult.

Day one of my first real job.

Day one with my first real boss.

Mere seconds ago, my new floor manager had pole-vaulted into a fluorescent-lit break room the size of a prison cell and excitedly introduced himself, like a game show host, to our just-hired group of summer college employees, not a one of us looking as though we could even land a job stocking plastic belts at Benetton.

My new boss had pointed a stubby finger at his muddy brown, hard plastic name badge, in which he had manipulated the punch letters of his real name by alternately crossing out, Magic Markering, and adding new ones—like it was a craft project—artfully transforming his nametag to now read "Sean R.S."

"Ssshhhee?" He pointed once more.

No one laughed. Out loud. Instead, we all stared at each other, panicked yet amused, trying to act like mature adults. Sean R.S had a lisp. A pretty bad one, the spray kind, like a cooling mister at a water park.

"Get it? Yeesshhh!" He was growing impatient.

This time, we all laughed uncomfortably, in that *Holy shit! We're doomed!* sort of way, like when a doctor with very cold hands asks you to turn your head and cough.

Sean R.S began quickly scanning everyone's nametags, before stopping on mine.

"And you are . . . ? Wade R. Oh my God! Wader!" he yelled in my face. His breath smelled like egg salad. And Bubble Yum. "Wader. Perfect abbreviation. We'll get along *ssshhhwimmingly*."

I was drenched.

He waited in anticipation once more, excitedly covering his mouth with the back of his hand as he laughed. He started to bellow ghoulishly, a mix of Dracula and Paul Lynde.

Again, no one laughed.

"Doesshhn't anyone get it?" he asked our group disappointedly. "Wader . . . water . . . ssssshhhwimmingly."

I looked around and studied my new retail family, which remained silent, except for a few nervous twitters. Our uninspired, comatose workforce was comprised mostly of college-age kids, like me, who only wanted a job that would pay them enough to stay on campus for the summer, eat ramen noodles, and drink twelve-packs of Meisterbräu every night. I couldn't go home this summer; I wanted to prove I was a semi-adult, capable of earning my first steady paycheck and showing up on time for something other than happy hour. Mostly, I just wanted to get drunk.

In an odd twist of fate, this was the only summer job I could land, here, at Sears, the location of much of my childhood trauma, the land of my Husky-wearing youth, the place that served as my house of fashion for years. I was once a Winnie-the-Pooh clothing model; then I became a Husky; and, now, I was a Sears employee. It all made sense, in a David Lynch sort of way.

"*No one* getssshh it?" Sean R.S asked again.

I couldn't take the painful silence and I wanted to laugh badly anyway, so I squeaked out an obligatory giggle at his lame joke, and everyone in our pathetic little group turned to laser their hatred on me.

"Suck up," the girl straddling the folding chair next to me whispered.

I gave her the look; the mean one I used in college to wither my opponents. "Nice lace gloves," I mouthed, looking at her nametag. "*Toni C.*"

Last names, I quickly learned, were not used anywhere in retail, like witness protection.

Toni C. giggled at my insult, her chair squeaking. I instantly liked her. Toni C. looked just like Madonna in *Desperately Seeking Susan*. If Madonna had eaten Rosanna Arquette. Toni was a big girl who was sporting really damaged, overprocessed hair.

"I think we'll get along *ssshhhwimmingly*," she whispered to me.

I laughed out loud, releasing a snort.

"No joking around," Sean R.S said. "Retail ish ssshherious businessh."

But I had no idea just how serious.

Just a few minutes later, our sad little group was simply tossed into the world of retail, slowly going mad under the hum of dim fluorescent lighting and Muzak and children screaming and women asking if this was really a size 16 while eating Cheetos out of their purses, and the sounds of cash registers and phones ringing and table saws being demonstrated and paint being shaken.

3

And yet, despite the insanity, I would also learn in my few short, hectic weeks the business skills that would eventually carry me to great success in my future PR career.

Learn from my example, children.

Multitasking

Decades before the term "multitasking" was in vogue, I owned it. In retail, you see, what you are hired to do and what you actually do are two entirely different things.

I would find out too late it was like that with every job.

I was *officially* hired to work in men's wear and children's wear, assisting customers with their purchases, helping them locate an item, working the cash register. I was not told that I would also serve as a counselor, shrink, liar, babysitter, and construction worker.

My first day a woman who looked like Lulu Roman from *Hee Haw* asked me what was wrong with the sizes.

"Ummm . . . what do you mean?" I asked her. She was my first official customer. In women's wear. Toni C. had asked me to cover for her while she went on break.

"I'm a 10, porkchop," Lulu said, losing a hand in her frosted, permed mane that looked like it was orbiting her head. "But I'm having trouble squeezing into a 16."

Now, I didn't know women's sizes, but I knew my mother was around a 6/8, and this woman was, at least, three times as big. Not counting her head.

"Let me look into that," I said.

I sprinted around the floor in desperation, looking for help, before running directly into Toni C., who had returned from break but had not informed me of that. She was busy . . . busy publicly humiliating a few mannequins, pulling their blouses down to reveal plastic, nipple-free breasts.

"Tear the labels out," she told me, without looking up.

"What? I can't do that. That would be defacing the merchandise. And lying."

"When I ask you what size I am, you better say a 10. Now I know I'm not, but you tell me I am. Get it? Haven't you ever dated a girl? Oh . . . now, shoo, I'm busy."

Toni C. then proceeded to unbutton a shirt and tie it in the back, leaving a topless torso to greet Sears's shoppers.

I ran back to Lulu and told her there was, indeed, a recent resizing of the merchandise. "European fit," I whispered.

She nodded, angrily but knowingly.

"What are you interested in trying on?" I asked.

She shoved a pile of size 10, bedazzled, Nashville-inspired duds in my hands. I told her to wait in a fitting room, and, while she was hidden away, I replaced her size 10s with size 20s, ripping the labels out before I handed them over the door to her.

She emerged, spinning, pleased, like Cheryl Tiegs.

"I knew it!" she yelled.

Still later that first day, I was asked to cover for a delinquent employee in tools, asked, I know, because I was one of the few men working nearby. I was instantly panicked, considering I didn't know the difference between a flathead and Phillipshead, between a circular saw and a rototiller.

"Where's yur ratchet doodle-dads and mish-mash flidgetty widgets?" asked a man who looked like he had just built a pickup from scratch. Using his teeth.

"Excuse me?" I asked.

"Where's yur ratchet doodle-dads and mish-mash flidgetty widgets. I'm in a hurry."

I smiled. Of course, this wasn't what he had said, but what I heard. Halfway through college, and my vocabulary had minimized instead of expanding. It had now become limited to the words "wasted," "Wham!," and "party." I tried to have a rather manly college fraternity brother of mine teach me about plumbing, in case I ever found myself in a situation like this, but he had lost interest when I kept singing "Careless Whisper" into a pipe.

I knew *nada* about tools.

"Let me get someone, sir," I said, grabbing a man with dirty hands who looked like he had worked in hardware for decades.

I stood close by, a bit envious, listening to these two men talk excitedly about HVAC systems and rebar and wrenches and screws. But as the conversation dragged on, I thought seriously but briefly about sawing off my hand when they began picking up chainsaws, before Toni C. saved my ass.

"Emergency in children's wear," she said.

And there was.

Minutes later, I was rearranging hundreds of little girl's dresses, which had been knocked off a series of rounders by twin girls who looked like dachshunds, while Toni C. dressed a series of mannequins to look like Lisa Lisa and Cult Jam, adding some eye shadow "to give them depth."

And this was the first lesson I learned in retail, as I watched Toni C. perform plastic makeovers while I meticulously sorted dresses: Don't take your job too seriously, or you'll go crazy.

Long Lunch Breaks

When all of this got to be too much—which was about ten times a day—Toni C. and I would take our break. Whether we had one coming or not.

The best thing about working retail—beside the store discount—were the breaks. In fact, extending lunch hour, taking a break, chatting on the phone with friends, balancing your checkbook were pretty much the best part of every job I would ever have. My dad called it "wasting company time" or "featherbedding." I called it "making the day fly."

Nearly every break, Toni C. and I would sprint to the food court, where we would eat Sbarro's and leer at the boys who worked there. I loved the food court, the buzz and the excitement of the thin, tan kids who got to lie by the pool all day and then show up at the mall around four o'clock to shop and go to a matinee movie.

Toni C. and I would sit and listen to "Sussudio" blaring over the speakers in the food court, while leering at the Sbarro's boys. Though Toni C. and I never talked about my being gay, she quietly understood we shared a similar interest, namely, the pizza boys, who were Vinnie-Barbarino hot. It was like they were flown directly into my little college town straight from Brooklyn, like human *salsicha*—their appearance alone enough to make my mouth water. So I mainlined Sbarro's, neutralizing the greasy, canoe-sized slices with diet soda. I would always dawdle until I could be served by "Billy Z.," as his nametag stated. Billy Z. looked like he just hopped off the set of *The Outsiders*. I tried to flirt as best as a fat, closeted boy could while ogling a living David, but it was a sad thing to watch.

"So, what's *hot* today, Billy?" I would ask, trying to sound subtly sexual but instead sounding like a complete jackass.

"Uhhh, what? Yeah, like, the pepperoni just came out of the oven."

Billy Z. said the same thing every day. His biceps were bigger than his IQ.

"Two slices of pepperoni and two diet sodas," Toni C. would answer, irritated. "My God, you're pathetic."

"Shut up and eat your pizza, bitch," I would snarl.

We were a sad twosome, the fat fag and the fat fag hag, who grew up in the wrong era, in a time when we knew nothing about carbs or trans fat, grew up mainlining Little Debbies and Hot Fries and Hostess apple pies from 7-Eleven.

"Oh my God, look at the Sears Queers!" the girls from Units would giggle, as they sashayed by our table.

I would duck my head, embarrassed, unable to stand up to these pretty girls for some unknown reason. It was so *not* me. But here, in the mall, I felt paralyzed, unworthy.

Toni C., however, was never intimidated. "Listen, bitches," she would say, grabbing them by their giant belts, jerking them around, like she was lassoing a calf. "You don't wanna fuck with me, got it, or you'll only be able to sip Orange Juliuses for a month."

The girls would scamper, and Toni C. would continue eating.

"I got your back, kid," she would say. "I'm not taking any shit. And you shouldn't either."

And it was from Toni C. I learned my second invaluable lesson: Surround yourself with strong women, girls who can not only stand up for themselves, but, most importantly, girls who can also kick someone's ass for you when you need it.

8

Dress for Success

I always wanted to dress like a winner, like Judd Nelson in *St. Elmo's Fire*. I knew that how you looked influenced people. Our fraternity took the great-looking guys who dressed like great-looking guys. I squeezed by on my sarcastic humor. And my ability to drink thirty beers without dying.

I owned only a few nice pieces of clothing because I didn't like the way I looked in clothes. When I looked in the mirror, I wanted to *see* thin, but when I looked I saw only fat.

Most days at Sears, I wore hand-me-downs from my much thinner father: a paper-thin, white cotton, button-down shirt that stretched over my man breasts to reveal brown dinner-plate nipples; polyester ties the size of canoe paddles; a gold-buttoned blue blazer, which looked like a shrug on my hunched, oversized shoulders. And my trousers were supposed to have pleats and, ideally, a belt that was supposed to be visible to the public, but my ever-ballooning weight had made those fashion feats impossible. Still, I thought, *Yes, fashion is where I should be! I will learn!*

And I did.

Within a week, Toni C. taught me fashion was as much a state of mind as a location.

"I'd kill to work at Benetton," she told me, "but I don't think they would ever hire me. But I don't let that stop me from dressing in style. You need to think the same thing."

Toni C. became my own personal Patricia Field, styling me in the latest trends. She helped me buy razor-thin leather ties, and Polo sweaters, and clothes that helped thin me and make me look like I wasn't jaundiced. I helped her scour for Madonna retreads that would actually fit.

I hadn't lost any weight, despite the fact I subsisted mostly on ramen noodles. But I now knew how to disguise my weight better; and that gave me confidence.

"That boy just gave you a double take," Toni C. told me one day, behind the register, when a pack of gay guys herded through Sears. Toni C. was one of the first people to be honest with me, to talk to me like being gay was OK.

"You're insane!"

"He did. He's doing it again."

I turned, and a thin boy with a just a touch of eye makeup and a Flock of Seagulls hairdo smiled at me. I turned back toward the register, mortified. This had never happened to me.

"Have some confidence, boy!" Toni C. told me. "It's all about confidence. Even fat girls get laid."

Nothing happened that day, of course, but that single moment—the first boy to smile at *me*—gave me hope. I had learned lesson three: Dressing could make the man.

I'd cross the undressing part of the bridge when I came to it. About a decade later.

Brownnosing

Every day, Sean R.S would bound onto the floor like a gymnast and scream, with his sad little lisp, "It'sssshhh a glorioussshhh day, Sshheearrss employeessshhh! Let'sss ssssheell with a ssshhmillle!"

"Let's sell without drowning the customers," Toni C. would always say, a bit too loudly.

Although I didn't like Sean R.S, I didn't hate him either. I felt sorry for him, wondered how, in his thirties, he had ended up here and yet seemed absolutely fine with the final outcome, like many of these shoppers who came to the mall looking like they didn't even have a mirror in their homes. I was nice to Sean R.S, much to the chagrin of my co-workers. I didn't know how it would help me, but I knew being mean could only hurt me. And him.

Sean R.S liked me out of default, simply because I acknowledged his existence. I would bring him coffee when I got some and talk to him about my studies, and he would ask how "ssshaaalesss" were going. I would always say "swimmingly," and smile, while Toni C. would always say "ssshhhwimmingly," and giggle. I didn't know if he were married, or had children, or dated; we never talked about any subjects in depth. We were alike in that way, sticking to safe topics—like the weather, what we had for breakfast—that never revealed too much. Loneliness is too sad a conversational topic.

Nearly every day, I was late to work. And, nearly every day, I forgot to lay away the layaway, simply leaving it shoved under the counter. And nearly every day, I answered the phone "Yeah?" once too often, came to work hung over, and could never quite get the hang of how to charge something. And yet Sean R.S never lost his patience. He was trying to teach me something: courtesy to customers, enthusiasm for your job, respect for your co-workers, responsibility. He was trying to teach me to be a grown-up. But I wasn't ready for that. I felt college-boy superior, smarter than him, and smug about my future success. I didn't need this gig, I thought, but he did.

And then one day, I came within an inch of bitch-slapping a little girl for knocking dresses off of rounders after I'd spent all day arranging them by size, color, and style. I had been "overserved" once again the night before, and I was depressed, after having eaten an entire Domino's pizza at two in the morning. So when this little girl wrecked an entire day of work in roughly three minutes—after eating colored candies and leaving red, yellow, and blue fingerprints like a bad criminal all over the aqua- and daffodil-dyed frocks—I lost it. I hid in a rounder and scared the shit out of her. Then she pointed out the "bad man" to her mother, and her mother did the same to Sean R.S.

And it was then that Sean R.S taught me the final and yet most valuable lesson of all: When you have a bad employee, you have to get rid of him, no matter how much you may like him. That's what grown-ups do. Because they have to.

"You're a good person," Sean R.S told me. "But you're a terrible employee. You need to be both in this world. Good luck."

I was gone. Not fired, really, but not asked to stay around.

So I simply left.

But the retail lessons I learned never did.

The Final Facial
Stewart Lewis

"Do you consider yourself a leader?"

That was the first question I was asked in an interview for a retail job at Drop, a boutique and spa in Manhattan.

"Completely," I answered. "I got 'most likely to succeed' in fifth grade." I realized that was probably the most inane thing I could have said at that moment, and wiped at my brow. The woman interviewing me was short and curvy with bad highlights and breasts that were so pert I couldn't stop staring at them. She was the type of woman that had so much work done she could have been forty or seventy, I had no clue.

"We are at the forefront of the spa industry," she said, "worldwide."

Clearly, I thought. How else could she have bought that face?

"That's great."

"What do your parents do?" she asked.

What did my parents have to do with selling eye cream and scheduling time-freeze facials?

"My mother is a teacher, and my father passed away."

"Oh, I'm sorry to hear that."

"Yes."

Yes? What question was I answering?

I had just turned thirty-four and it was quite possibly my

most humiliating moment. I was clamoring, even sweating, in front of Miss Day Spa. I was desperate for a job, trying to dumb myself down but coming across as a tool.

"Would you consider yourself a moody person?"

"I generally tend to check my baggage at the door."

Finally, a well-rounded answer.

Miss Day Spa let out a pretentious little chuckle and straightened her lime green top.

"Well, to be honest, you do seem a bit overqualified."

You mean why the fuck does a masters-degreed graduate from a top writing school want to work for twelve an hour? Truth was, I had moved to New York with $2,000, which lasted about three weeks. In New York, it costs fifty bucks to breathe.

"Yes, but really, I just want to work hard in a nice environment while I work on my book—on my own time, of course."

Miss Day Spa studied her reflection in the mirror that lined her sleek, loft office. She looked like she was frozen in a wind tunnel, her skin in the act of leaving her face behind. It was frightening.

"Well, why don't you see Ariane and she'll do your paperwork."

That was it? I was hired?

My cell phone buzzed as I was shoved into an office in front of a computer and told to "hold on."

As a friend inquired about a dinner plan, I opened the Salon Biz software. I tried to think of a celebrity to search the database for. Susan Sarandon.

> Sarandon, Susan: Glycolic Facial with Iliana.
> 9/4/03 $160

"Are you listening to me?" my friend wanted to know.

"Susan Sarandon," I said.

"Yes, love her. Why?"

"Glycolic facial. Gotta go." The thought of working with celebrities was maybe worth it. Maybe.

I hung up as a pale, emaciated girl walked in, put down her deli coffee, and sat down.

"Hi, I'm Nancy," came a thin, raspy voice.

I shook her hand very carefully so as not to crack the bones. She was abnormally peppy, especially since during the seven hours that she trained me on the Salon Biz software she did not eat anything—the only thing she ingested was the last sip of her cold coffee.

I went to the spa the next day and trained with the manager Melanie, who also had fake breasts. She was Chinese, and from Miami, which explained her Columbian accent. I couldn't believe she was running a high-end spa, but barely spoke English.

"Joo don no, girl," she said while rearranging some $40 candles. She assumed I was gay right away (do straight guys work in spas?) and therefore felt free to refer to me as a female.

"Dis place, I can get any ting done."

I didn't know if she meant that she *can* get anything done or *can't* get anything done, so I just nodded. For the entire shift, she hardly trained me, just talked while applying lip-gloss and pencil and occasionally eating from a box of jelly donuts hidden in a drawer. She went next door twice during the day to try on some Nine West shoes, which she finally bought the third time, leaving me alone at the desk for fifteen minutes during which a lady came in to exchange a $100 gift certificate for two express manicure/pedicures and pay the balance in cash. I was completely flustered, especially because the security guard was pestering me about something with only bits of English flecked into the information.

"You're going to have to wait." I said to Pablo. "Wait."

The lady had a droopy, accusatory face and a tiny little black poodle that was licking her ear. She looked at me like I was an alien.

"I'm sorry, I am train—"

"This is ridiculous—we have to go. Where's Melanie?"

"*We* have to go?"

"She has a poodle party around the corner."

Oh, the dog. I could just see it. Poodles in Prada, sipping Perrier in Gramercy Park. It was all too "day spa" for me. I tried to breathe along with the droning single-note cello and water-fall soundtrack coming from the nearly invisible Bang and Olufsen speakers.

"Where is she!?"

I felt like telling the lady to take her poodle and her $140 French wrinkle cream and shove it up her Upper East Side. But I opted for the customer service approach.

"She won't be a minute, I'm afraid she is the only one who can authorize the transaction."

Mrs. Greenblatt and her poodle both scowled at me and made a brisk, dramatic exit.

That night I cried in the shower. Was this my future? Dealing with evil poodle ladies every day? I went out that night and drank four martinis and kissed a Monet on the dance floor. It was an escape, not a solution.

On my second day Melanie informed me that we get 15 per-cent commission on anything we sold in the spa boutique, so when a woman was dropped off by a driver in a tinted, black stretch limo, I was thinking *mattress* (I was sleeping on a futon, something that is hip for a dorm, but forbidden for anyone over thirty). She came in and lifted her Gucci sunglasses to rest on her head and started perusing the little couture purses we had in a glass case.

"Aren't they *très* precious?" I said.

"Mmm," she replied, as if they tasted like sorbet.

An hour later, I had sold her $2,500 in merchandise—not bad for my second day. I threw in some lip plumper gratis. My hangover didn't seem so bad.

Miss Stretch Limo was a prime example of a rich person not yet corrupted by an excess of money. She was a newbie, and enjoying it. I gave her a hug, and Melanie frowned.

"Joo don't touch the customer."

"She just spent a fortune honey, I should *go down* on her."

Melanie laughed.

"Joo funny," she said.

I told her about Mrs. Greenblatt and she rolled her eyes.

"She crazy."

As I unpacked the diamond-studded dog collars and pot-pourri, I was thinking a thought that most people in retail think: This is a means to an end. I smelled expensive lavender soap on two beautiful women walking past me and thought: Soon enough I'll be one of them, working my savage St. Barths tan in December, buying a ten-session chunk of oxygen facials like they were M&Ms.

The three typical clients at Drop:

1. Forty-something women getting Brazilian waxes on their way to exotic locations

2. Sixty-something women with tiny dogs getting manicures

3. Jewish guys getting their backs waxed

One particular guy, obviously there by order from his despot wife, would rather have been switching between lesbian porn and a Yankees game, clutching a cold beer, than in a spa. He had so much hair poking out of every orifice that even a dream team of Nordic estheticians couldn't begin to quell it. Face it, I wanted to say, you're a chimp. The only person you should be getting intimate with is Jane fucking Goodall.

But who was I to judge? That day I was sporting a whitehead on my nose that had grown in diameter after the Mrs. Greenblatt incident. Working in a spa makes you notice everybody's imperfections, including your own. I began to gauge how far from a mirror I had to be so that my crow's feet wouldn't be noticed, and then put myself that distance from everyone.

"Wuz wrong? Do I smell?" Melanie wanted to know. "Come! I show you close out."

All the employees at Drop had something else they were "working on." I had recently submitted my novel to a publisher and was "waiting" for a response. Just like Melanie was "waiting" to get her commercial agent and Jerod was "waiting" for enough savings to go find his ex-boyfriend in Australia. But what then? Wasn't there was always a higher dream, something else to yearn for?

One day, while it was slow, I had one of the girls give me a pedicure. Her name was Luisa, and she traveled two hours to get to work, just to clean people's fingers and toes. It made my futon situation seem more bearable. Afterwards, I gave her a large bag of designer chocolates and her smile beamed off her face. It made me wonder if I really wanted to be on the other side of the reservation desk. Most of the rich people I knew weren't happy. There was always something to complain about. I remembered something my ex-boyfriend Barkley had told me years before. He was a millionaire and had taken me to a posh resort in Mexico. When we went into town, we passed a bunch of locals on a shabby strip of beach. They were singing, and drinking, and laughing. You could tell they had nothing—they were probably going to sleep right where they were—but I'd never seen a group of people so happy.

"Do me a favor," Barkley said, "never get rich."

It was a random comment said in passing, but the meaning of it was still sinking in. Here in the spa, the people that came in to get treatments, buy overpriced items, and feel better about themselves were of a certain tax bracket, one that everyone seemed to be striving for. I always loved material things and being pampered, but I enjoyed them more because they came in short bursts—it wasn't a continual thing.

I expressed my theory to Melanie.

"Joo kidding? I want bling girl. I want a giant rock on my finger and a closet full of Prada."

"Well, so do I of course, but I'm starting to reconsider."

The following week, while it was slow, I had Iliana give me a facial. She told me I had a lot of blackheads and I was slightly mortified. As the mask was drying on my face I heard an argument outside the treatment room. Then the door burst open and Miss Day Spa was inches away from me, fuming.

"What in God's name do you think you're doing? During your shift? Get out!"

Iliana was standing behind her with her arms crossed, mumbling in Swedish. I pointed to the mask on my face.

"Out!"

Well, apparently I was fired—mid-facial. I grabbed my coat and my scarf and walked by Melanie at the desk who whispered, "Don worry, joo better off."

On the subway home my face started cracking. People gave me looks that said: *freak*. The mask was still on—it had all happened so fast. All the employees got treatments when it was slow, why had it been me that was busted?

The answer lay in a grey piece of paper on top of my futon.

That publisher called, they want you to call them ASAP!

I called before I had even washed the mask off.

"We would love to publish your manuscript," the voice said.

After washing the mask off, I saw a different face. It was a face that was going somewhere. I knew that one could hardly make a living in New York as a writer, but I also knew that my advance would buy me some breathing room. I didn't necessarily want to be as rich as Mrs. Greenblatt, but I was thankful to not have to rely on the spa for a paycheck. Buh-bye retail, hello book tour.

Minimum-Wage Drama
Elaine Viets

The first rule of retail is that everyone wants to check out at once. I can stand at my cash register for half an hour without a single customer. Suddenly, by some hidden signal, everyone in the bookstore will get in the checkout line.

I was facing one of those lines in a big chain bookstore in South Florida. Ten people, all looking at their watches.

The large, angry man in front of the line was cussing me out. "You're an idiot," he said. "These paperbacks are the same price. I'm taking this book back and getting this book instead. Why can't I just exchange them?"

He slammed the Tom Clancy novel on the counter.

"I'm sorry, sir," I said. "I need the manager's approval for a book exchange."

"It's a lousy six-dollar paperback." Now he was screaming, his face so red with rage I thought he might have a stroke. He pounded the countertop with the paperback.

Behind him, I could see the line getting longer and more restless.

"Manager to the front," I called on the store intercom. But the manager was tied up with a crisis in the bookstore café.

The man kept yelling at me. "Manager to the front," I pleaded. The line grew longer.

Then the woman behind him said, "I hate it when people don't take their medication."

The woman behind her said, "Rude people stink."

Soon all the women in line were talking about how much they hated public rudeness. Mr. Rude turned a shade redder.

At last, the bookstore manager ran up and punched in the approval code on my cash register. Mr. Rude grabbed his book and left.

The woman in line patted my hand and said, "You're doing a good job, honey. You hang in there."

That scene explains my love-hate relationship with retail. I've met some of the kindest, funniest people in stores. I've also met some of the rudest.

The angry man was indulging in a favorite customer pastime—clerk abuse. I'm amazed by the number of well-dressed, well-educated men and women who take out their frustrations by yelling at underpaid clerks. They have a bad day at the office or a fight with their spouse and take it out on us.

These people know we're helpless. If I wanted to keep my job, I had to keep my mouth shut. I had to have this job. I was doing research for my Dead-End Job mystery series.

How many times have you heard retail workers say, "I ought to write a book about this place?"

I really do. Like my series character, Helen Hawthorne, I actually work the jobs I write about, the ones that pay between $6 and $11 an hour.

I was a telemarketer for *Dying to Call You* and a hotel maid for *Murder With Reservations*. But my retail jobs provide real drama for the series. Working retail is like going to the theater—except you get paid to watch the show. Also, your feet hurt.

For the first book in the series, *Shop Till You Drop*, I worked at a high-priced dress shop. I encountered everything from very young women with very old boyfriends to female flashers to clever shoplifters.

One woman shoplifter worked the mall with a baby in a stroller. She would walk into a store and pinch the baby. While the bawling baby distracted the staff, she would stuff expensive dresses into a diaper bag. She was finally caught by security. She no longer pinches dresses—or babies.

For *Murder Between the Covers*, I worked at a bookstore. Bookselling was the one retail job I'd do again. It's a useful profession in a world that has too many useless ones. We don't need another overpriced dress shop. We can definitely do without telemarketers. But I loved selling books. I liked their smell, their feel, their colorful covers neatly lined up on the shelves, promising order and intelligence. I enjoyed finding the right book for a customer: It was literary matchmaking.

People ask, "Why didn't you just interview booksellers?"

Unless you've been on your feet eight hours and have the varicose veins to prove it, you don't understand bookselling. Until your back hurts from hauling books, you're not a bookseller.

Working in a bookstore was hard labor. Hardcovers weigh a pound or more. Hauling them around the store was like moving paving stones.

Customers often demanded, "Why isn't someone waiting on me?"

I can answer that question. The booksellers were running around, putting away the books that customers left all over the store. Every day, the average chain store has to reshelve several hundred books and magazines.

The one question I could never answer was why the *Kama Sutra* always wound up in the pregnancy section.

Was working in a bookstore really a dead-end job? It was when I was behind the cash register. I was the slowest clerk in the system, even if I did get a twenty-five-cent raise for being a "team player."

Working on the other side of the cash register gave me a different view of the world. Take the customer who said, "I'm looking for a book. I can't remember the name. I don't know the author. But the cover was blue."

How often had I asked for a book in that same vague way? I used to say something like, "It was a mystery, it had 'death' in the title, and I think the author was interviewed on NPR."

Now I was on the other side of the counter, trying to answer this impossible request.

I was fascinated by the strange dramas that happen in retail. Once, a drunken numismatist brought in her coin collection to pay for some magazines. With shaking hands, she counted out $24.27, dropping pennies and nickels all over the counter and floor. Customers rushed to retrieve them. They knew they wouldn't be waited on until she paid.

A pair of witches bought a book of spells at our store. I don't know about you, but I wouldn't buy spells in a suburban bookshop. What could you do—make enchanted door wreaths?

When I rang up the witches' book, I hit the wrong key. The register jammed. Another bookseller, Jeremy, tried to help me and we double-jammed my register. The witches frowned and played with their pentagrams.

"If they turn me into a frog, it's your fault," I whispered to Jeremy.

"Don't worry," he said. "I know some witches who can undo spells."

He wasn't kidding.

Then there was the man with the black beard and eyes like twin pools of tar. He came up to my counter and said, "I want to return this."

The book was called *How to Cast Out Devils*. I was afraid to ask why he was returning it. I didn't know which scared me more: if the book worked—or if it didn't.

In addition to enjoying the customers, I got a real kick out of my colleagues. One favorite was Brad, who worked in the magazine department.

Brad was in an unending battle against the magazine insert cards. The white postage-paid cards covered the bookstore floor like snow. No matter how many times a day Brad picked them up, there were always more insert cards on the carpet.

One day, Brad had enough. He collected a huge stack of the cards and dropped them in the mail. He didn't fill out the cards. He just mailed them. "If the magazines want to hear from me, well, they will," he said. "But they'll pay for the privilege."

I've heard that other booksellers now follow Brad's practice since my book came out.

For high emotion, there was my stint in the bridal department at Zola Keller, on fashionable Las Olas Boulevard in Fort Lauderdale. Zola's was the kind of store where people spent a quarter of a million dollars on a wedding. I once saw a fight between a husband and wife in the store. The woman came out of the dressing room in a nice blue mother-of-the-bride dress.

"How much is that dress?" her husband demanded.

"Five hundred dollars," the wife said.

"Don't you ever come out in a cheap dress again. You make me look bad. You must spend at least three thousand dollars."

I'm still waiting for a fight like that with my husband.

There really is a Zola Keller, and she is a diplomat of the first order. One day, a bride came into the store and wanted to see her bridesmaids' dresses. These were beautiful, frothy creations in celadon. When you spend five thousand bucks on a dress, you don't call it celery green.

The bride pulled out two carpet fibers, held them against the dress and burst into tears.

"They don't match," the bride wailed. "They're two shades off. The dresses are supposed to match the hotel carpet."

This was a crisis I couldn't handle. I ran for Zola.

"What's the problem?" she asked the bride.

"My dresses don't match the carpet," the bride said. "My wedding is ruined."

"They're not supposed to match," Zola said. "That's so Kmart. Didn't you see *Vogue*? They're supposed to be two shades off."

The bride stopped weeping and held the fibers to the dress again. "They're exactly two shades," she said. "You've saved my wedding."

I also saw scenes of great beauty at Zola's. One African American bride glided down the fitting room stairs, a vision in her wedding dress and veil. Her mother, a well-known gospel singer, burst into song. That scene brought tears to my eyes.

Another bride came in for a final fitting for her wedding

gown. "Put on your veil," her mother said.

The young bride did. Her mother wept. "My daughter's really getting married," she said. "Without the veil, it was only a prom dress."

Working retail could make you into a philosopher. For *Murder Unleashed*, I did my research at a high-end dog boutique in Fort Lauderdale called Bone Appetit.

This is the world where people spend $200 for a dog birthday party. Mark Tews, one of the store's owners, told me, "Little dogs are babies, big dogs are pals."

He was right. I'd see guys come in with their big Labradors. They would ride together in the pickup truck, share beer and burgers, and shed on the couch. They were pals.

I'd also see women carry around little white dogs like babies. One woman had three teenagers. "This dog keeps me sane," she said. "It's the only thing on earth that obeys me."

One of the women who came into the store looked like Paris Hilton twenty years later. She had a young man with her who I thought was her son, home from college.

She picked up a spiked dog collar, suitable for a large Doberman, and said, "I want this—for him."

"Uh," I said.

Mark the owner came rushing over. "No, no. You don't want that. Everyone gets that for their boy toys. Get the plain black leather."

I wondered what kind of world she lived in where everyone had spiked collars for their boy toys.

The dogs at this store had more clothes than I did. I really wanted the pink sweater that said BITCH in rhinestones. But I wasn't ready to wrestle a Doberman for it.

My favorite dog was Lulu, a low-slung beagle-dachshund. Lulu owned Mark Tews. She modeled the dog clothes at the store, and swanked around in little embroidered sundresses or feather boas.

She got the care a supermodel deserved. I would be cleaning up after incontinent Chihuahuas and hear, "Lulu, time for your manicure." Lulu got two manicures and a massage every week.

Lulu only bit one customer. The man came in for dog food, but he couldn't remember the brand. He called his wife on his cell phone and said loudly, "Hey, are you in bed or on the can?"

Lulu gave him a tiny nip.

Mark the owner apologized profusely. I sneaked Lulu a treat. I would have bit the guy if I could have gotten away with it.

I'm now on my sixth Dead-End Job book. There seems to be an endless supply of retail work. I just hope there's an endless supply of readers.

Fortunately, one memory from my time in retail cheers me up. It answers the question, "Does anyone still read?"

Let me take you back to the bookstore one more time.

Two boys came up to my cash register. One was about eight, the other around twelve years old. The eight-year-old had a copy of *The Adventures of Captain Underpants*. If you're not familiar with that series, eight-year-old boys love it. It's full of bathroom jokes. Parents hate it. Grandparents buy for their grandchildren to irritate their proper sons and daughters.

The eight-year-old put the book on the counter along with a crumpled ten. This was clearly his allowance money.

I asked the twelve-year-old, "Are you a *Captain Underpants* fan?"

"That's for kids," he said. "Ever hear of Steinbeck?"

"Yes," I said.

"Ever read *The Grapes of Wrath*?" he said.

"Yes."

"Steinbeck rules," he said.

Steinbeck rules. I think about that on bad days. That is the future: Steinbeck rules.

Un Posto Speciale (A Special Place)
Jim DeRogatis

Al Rocky's Music Store never seemed to have any customers, but that never seemed to bother Al Rocky. I found him in the same place whenever I walked in after school, sitting on a rickety wooden stool behind the big steel cash register that never rang. Al talked in a raspy but mellifluous voice that evoked the flow of notes from the worn clarinet he sometimes pulled from behind the counter, where other shopkeepers in the neighborhood would have kept their baseball bats. Occasionally, he lapsed into Italian, usually at the end of recounting an oft-told tale from his days with the big band legend Gene Krupa.

Al's two cronies sat on aluminum and nylon-webbing folding chairs on the other side of the register. I never learned their names, but I'm pretty sure that one of them was alternately called Giuseppe/Joe. In any group of Italian American men their age in Jersey City, New Jersey, there was bound to be a Giuseppe/Joe.

The three men sported the same growth of blotchy grey stubble; they wore the same Haband elastic-waist comfort-fit slacks, and they favored pink or yellow button-down Oxford shirts besmirched with tomato sauce and underarm stains. Al's two buddies were distinguished by the fact that one always wore a black fedora, and the other (Giuseppe/Joe) had survived a battle with throat cancer that left him with one of those creepy, metal-lic-sounding voice boxes. It required him to hold a small micro-phone to his Adam's apple when he spoke, which he rarely did, except when he cheered Al on.

"The bassist was always sweet on dat hat-check gal at Birdland," Al would say.

"DAT'S. RIGHT. AL," Giuseppe concurred in his mechanical drone.

A single fluorescent fixture hung from the pressed-tin ceiling and illuminated the pale green walls. The smell of stale cigar smoke hung over the drab ten-by-twelve storefront, though I never saw any of the men smoking cigars. They usually tucked a folded copy of the *New York Daily News* or the *Jersey Journal* under their arms, though I never saw them reading. I imagine they bought the papers to check on the ponies, or maybe to scan the numbers. From time to time, they sipped black coffee from blue-and-white takeout cups adorned with the Greek Parthenon and purchased from the Eagle Beef butcher shop down the block. Al usually celebrated the end of a tale by spiking everyone's coffee with a shot of anisette.

Al's stories never had much of a point, but his cronies seemed to enjoy hearing them as much as he enjoyed telling them. I just nodded obligingly.

"She was a looker, dat gal," Al would say. "But classy. Very classy."

"DAT'S. RIGHT. AL."

"Una signora molto distinta—e bello!"

And with that Al would uncork the bottle.

I discovered Al Rocky's by thumbing through the yellow pages; it was the only music store within walking distance of my home in the Jersey City Heights. I'd been sold on the idea of forming a band with two of my friends and fellow freshmen at Hudson Catholic Regional High School for Boys. Billy Texas (his real and unbelievably cool name) played some guitar, and John Tkaczyk claimed to play the bass. Every prospective band needs a drummer, and they anointed me.

Already well on my way to becoming an obsessive rock fan, I had never thought about actually making music, but John had already tried and failed to master the drums, and he loaned me an oversized pair of marching sticks, a wood-and-rubber practice pad, and a Mel Bay method book. Slowly and deliberately, I began tip-tapping my way through the rudiments, the core patterns of drumming technique, most of which have charmingly onomatopoeic names like flam, ruff, ratamacue, and paradiddle.

Left left right right left. Right right left left right. Monotonous at best, mind-numbingly boring at worst, my friends assured me that the hours of practice would pay off: Being in a band is the best way to meet girls, they said.

I continued practicing long after John gave up and the three of us stopped hanging out, because I really had nothing better to do, and paradiddling in the basement was at least a way to alleviate my fourteen-year-old-kid frustrations. The only girls I ever met came into Thom McAnn's on Central Avenue, where I worked part-time selling shoes after school and on the weekends. Brown suede Earth shoes outsold everything else because they were an approved alternative to the uniform saddle shoes at Saint Dominic Academy and Saint Michael's High School for Girls, where sneakers were strictly forbidden. I'd enthusiastical-

33

ly fetch the faux Hush Puppies from the wall and either hand them to the girls or, on especially lucky occasions, kneel down as beckoned to slip a pair onto rainbow-sock-covered feet as the body above did its best to ignore me. I certainly couldn't be any less cool or more invisible playing in a rock band.

In the late sixties and early seventies, my stepfather played the drums and sang with a small group that gigged at go-go bars in Union City and up and down the Jersey Shore. By the time I enrolled at Saint Nicholas Grammar School, he was teaching science and gym and playing acoustic guitar at folk masses, leading his seventh- and eighth-grade classes in rounds of "This Little Light of Mine." His drums were covered with a shiny black-and-white veneer called Black Diamond Pearl, Slingerland's version of the sparkle finish on Ringo's Ludwigs at the height of Beatlemania. The drums sat covered in dust amid the spare desks and broken chalkboards in an attic storeroom at Saint Nick's, and after a few months on the practice pad, I asked if I could borrow them. Twenty-four years later, I still haven't returned them.

The drums were made at the Slingerland factory in Niles, Illinois, in 1964, the year I was born. The bass drum and mounted tom-tom were sized for a small jazz set, but to me they seemed gigantic. In the style of Gene Krupa, the front bass drumhead was adorned with a crested logo bearing my stepdad's initials: HWR. He joked that they stood for Harry "Wonderful" Reynolds, though his mother had actually given him the middle name Prince William after a soap opera character she loved. I couldn't blame him for losing the *P*.

As I rummaged through the attic, I also found a wobbly drum stool with a flat red seat; a flimsy, rusted, chrome cymbal stand; a squeaky Ludwig Speed King bass drum pedal; an old twenty-inch Avedis Zildjian ride cymbal; and a pair of Turkish-made Zildjian high-hat cymbals. The typical beginner's drum set includes all of these pieces, as well as a few others.

If you're right-handed, you hit the bass drum by stepping on the pedal with your right foot, providing the basic pulse of the music; in rock, it's the "one" and the "three." You press the high-hat pedal with your left foot, bringing the two cymbals together to create an accent at the same time that you use your left hand to hit the snare drum, which sits on a stand between your legs. This creates the alternating backbeat, or the "two" and the "four."

It takes some practice to coordinate and keep your balance, but it's like riding a bicycle, and in time you're moving forward with the most primal of rock rhythms. Your right hand generally "rides" or counts the time on the high-hat cymbals to your left or the big ride cymbal to your right, which hovers on a stand above the bass drum. The rack tom mounted above the bass drum and the deeper floor tom that rests on its own legs to your right are used for rhythmic accents—rolls or fills—which end with the punctuating strike of a second, smaller crash cymbal. Put it all together for two bars and it sounds like this:

> *one two three four / one two three four*
> *boom cha boom cha / boom cha bah-dum dum-crash!*

Once I'd hauled the mass of metal and wood home from Saint Nick's, I lovingly cleaned and polished it in the basement rec room with lemon-scented Pledge and foul-smelling Noxon. Assembling a drum kit—with its countless wing nuts, bolts, and heavy metal tubes—is like building something with a giant erector set, but I managed to put it all together based on the photos of Nick Mason and John Bonham in the oversized Pink Floyd and Led Zeppelin posters that I'd hung on the wood-paneled walls.

A drum set is unlike any other musical instrument: It envelops you, a world unto itself, like the cockpit of a racecar ready to be driven hard and fast. (Bonham's fantasy sequence in Zep's concert film *The Song Remains the Same* finds him zooming at 120 mph in a dragster.) I was hooked from the first time I sat on that shaky red stool, but I was missing the crash cymbal, the floor tom, and the snare drum—the very heart of the set, or its steering wheel. Someone had swiped these key pieces from the grammar school attic, so off to Al Rocky's I went.

Al didn't have much of an inventory. A smudgy glass counter wrapped around the back and right-hand walls of the store, and it held a few secondhand trumpets, flutes, and trombones, as well as assorted guitar cables, harmonicas, kazoos, penny whistles, plastic recorders, and an ancient red accordion. A warren of cubbyholes behind the register overflowed with replacement Remo drumheads, a Beatles songbook, stray pieces of sheet music, and wooden drumsticks neatly sorted by size and make. Three or four inexpensive new Cort and Harmony guitars hung on the left-hand wall, along with a half-dozen dirty, used cymbals. A cheap no-name black drum set occupied the front window.

Seasoned musicians would have walked in, taken one look around, and left, but I saw an entryway to a thoroughly mysterious and wonderfully seductive new world.

The first time I stopped by the shop, early in my freshman

year at Hudson Catholic, Al had closed up by the time I collected my Thom McAnn's paycheck and left work on Saturday. But as soon as class let out on Monday, I sprinted from school to Journal Square and rode the Central Avenue bus north to the seedy northern tip of the shopping strip, near the border of Union City.

The cronies were noncommittal, but Al took a liking to me from my first visit. For one thing, I stayed. For another, I left most of my paycheck behind, in exchange for a couple of pairs of Pro-Mark 5A nylon-tipped hickory drumsticks and that big Beatles songbook—useless to a drummer, but I figured I'd eventually meet some bandmates who could actually play, and it might come in handy for learning "Taxman" and "Hey Bulldog."

As I became a regular, I watched other kids my age come in and begrudgingly slam a few bucks on the counter for picks or patch chords that they would have lifted if not for the watchful eyes of Al's two shadows. Some of the teens sneered at Al behind his back because he was old and clueless and he didn't stock the sleek Ibanez guitars they'd seen advertised in the player's mags, though he had all of the glossy catalogs, and he always pledged that "I can order anything—an' wit' a big discount!"

Eventually I realized that there was another reason Al liked me: I listened to his stories as respectfully as his cronies did, and I pretended to be just as interested, when in truth it was everything in the store except for Al Rocky that fascinated me.

"Jimmy, I ever tell you about the place we'd play in Kansas City?" Al trilled.

"No, Mr. Rocky."

"Al. Call me Al. Damnedest place. Best steak I ever ate."

"Hmm."

I selected a new plastic bass drumhead to replace the one with my stepdad's initials, the better to claim the Slingerlands as my own.

"Used ta be drumheads were made a calfskin. Damn hard ta tune. Hadda hold a candle over 'em ta stretch 'em out."

"Oh, yeah?"

"Best steak ever. *Un posto speciale!*"

Rows of small, sticky wooden drawers like those in an old apothecary lined the wall behind the right-hand counter. Al let me have the run of the place, and I rummaged through these bins as he talked, marveling at the neatly separated plastic guitar picks, capos, and glass and brass slides; the spare tuning pegs, guitar and bass strings, and trumpet mutes; and most of all, the various and sundry drum parts: nuts, bolts, washers, replacement snares, screw-on bass drum spurs, a weird winged cymbal topper that turned any ride into a sizzle cymbal with little metal rivets that vibrated against the bronze, and round felt pads that protected the cymbals as they rested on the hard metal stands.

"Cymbal felts. You need cymbal felts? Take as many as you want. G'on."

"Thanks, Mr. Rocky."

"Al. Call me Al."

Like many accomplished musicians, Al knew a bit about drumming. Any other time, he moved in almost painful slow motion, like Mr. Tudball, the grizzled geezer Tim Conway played in skits on *The Carol Burnett Show*, but when he grabbed the sticks, his hands flew in a blur over the practice pad, bouncing and gliding through the flams, ruffs, ratamacues, and paradiddles in a way that mine never did.

"You try," Al said as he handed me the sticks and pushed the practice pad across the counter.

"Nah, Al. I just play the drums along with my rock records while I listen on headphones."

"Gotta walk before you can run, kid. *You try*."

I did, but only reluctantly, slow—clumsy and awkward in comparison to his fluid, graceful precision.

"'S alright, Jimmy. You keep at it. Gotta walk before you can run. *Keep at it*."

My first serious purchase at Al Rocky's came with the crisp $100 bill my mom gave me for my fifteenth birthday. Like the drums in the window, the bargain-basement snare that Al fished from the dark nether regions of the basement didn't have a name manufacturer, and its silver sparkle finish didn't match my inherited Slingerlands. It didn't matter: I finally had something to hit on "two" and "four."

It took me six more months to save up enough for a floor tom, which Al ordered from a distributor in Secaucus that supplied most of the inexpensive new gear that he stocked. I rode to the warehouse with him to pick it up. He hugged the wheel of his dented Chevy Impala, pressing his face as close to the windshield as possible, and maxing out at 30 mph on Routes 1 and 9 as the tractor-trailers thundered past. I tried to remember whether I'd seen him wearing glasses, and why he wasn't right now.

I had pictured the warehouse as a vast wonderland of shiny new instruments the likes of which I'd never seen, but we pulled up to a loading dock, rang a bell, and a big black teamster came out and handed us a bruised and battered cardboard box. The floor tom within was unscathed, and as I ripped it out of its plastic bag, I was even more excited than I'd been about the snare drum: It was bigger, it sort of matched the Slingerlands, and now I had the *dum dum* for my *bah-dum dum*. But I still lacked the second cymbal to provide that satisfying *crash!*

Seeing that I pored over them every time I visited, Al made the mistake of giving me the slick new Ludwig, Slingerland, and Zildjian catalogs midway through my junior year. I took them home and fantasized over them the way I did with the lending library of *Playboy*s and *Penthouse*s that circulated among my Hudson Catholic classmates. On the covers of my Mead notebooks, I drew elaborate diagrams of my dream drum set, a percussive arsenal to put the likes of Neal Peart and Carl Palmer to shame. Then I learned that there were stores that actually stocked this stuff to see, hear, caress, and, sometimes, even play, and they were just a thirty-cent PATH-train ride away on the other side of the Hudson River.

I forget who told me about the strip of Forty-eighth Street in Manhattan between Broadway and Fifth Avenue, or whether I first ventured there alone or in a group. On the north side of the street was a row of guitar shops filled with new and vintage axes. On the south were the two biggest music stores on the East Coast, Manny's and Sam Ash, as well as a few smaller and quirkier places like the Electro-Harmonix Hall of Science, which sold the company's effects pedals and produced a fifteen-minute concert complete with a light show on a small stage in the back to demonstrate the wares once an hour every Saturday.

I know that I bought my missing crash cymbal on Forty-eighth Street, and that I never made another major purchase at Al Rocky's, though I still returned—albeit less and less frequently—to pick up a pair of sticks or some more free cymbal felts. Al seemed more concerned about me losing the spark than he was about losing a customer.

"You keepin' at it, Jimmy? *Gotta keep at it.*"

He smiled when I assured him that I was.

"Good. I ever tell you about the place we played in Kansas City? Damnedest place. Best steak I ever ate."

I joined my first real band in the fall of 1982, at the beginning of my freshman year at New York University. We called ourselves the Interns, dressed in lime green surgical scrubs, and covered punk and new wave tunes such as "Submission" by the Sex Pistols, "I Wanna Be Sedated" by the Ramones, "What I Like About You" by the Romantics, and a medley of the three big hits by A Flock of Seagulls: "I Ran," "Space Age Love Song," and "Telecommunication."

Our guitarist, George Marrero, had graduated from Memorial High School in West New York and taken a job repairing X-ray equipment at a hospital in Elmhurst. (He was the source of our purloined scrubs.) Improbably thin, his favorite trick involved pulling up his shirt, sucking in his gut, and popping out his rib cage so that he looked like a concentration camp inmate. He could play scales on his cherry-red Fender Strat, smoke a fancy English cigarette, curse another driver in his thick Cuban accent (*"Me caquo en ti!"*), and simultaneously steer his company-issued Ford Fairmont station wagon at 70 mph through the Lincoln Tunnel by guiding the wheel with his bony brown knees.

We went to Forty-eighth Street together almost every Saturday. Once, we looked up to see the English new wave rocker Joe Jackson staring at the same Vox amplifier we'd been ogling. Another time, I ran into progressive-rock-god Carl Palmer in one of the drum departments. Spending money on Forty-eighth Street made me feel like a part of the same world the "real musicians" occupied in a way that Al Rocky's never did.

George spent the summer of '83 slowly building his ultimate effects board, adding another new pedal or electronic gizmo every few weeks, while I took advantage of my new part-time job at a brokerage on Wall Street to close in on my dream drum set. I'd already added a second crash cymbal, a tiny splash cymbal, a set of timbales (George's Latin influence), and a second mounted tom. George still needed an Electro-Harmonix Octave Multiplexer, and I yearned for a trio of Remo Rototoms—small, futuristic, high-pitched metal mini-drums that you tuned by turning the rims. We stood on the sidewalk staring at Manny's massive window display one sweltering afternoon in late August when a bearded, long-haired guy in a khaki Army jacket approached.

"You guys lookin' for a deal? Waddya need? I can get anything, half price."

He seemed cool; he was wearing a Rush T-shirt from the *Hemispheres* tour. George told him what he wanted.

"Fuck, man, no problem! You just gotta drive me to the warehouse."

George practically dragged the guy to the Fairmont. The Rush dude jumped in the front passenger's seat and directed George about a dozen blocks south and two blocks west. We double-parked in a loading zone beside a nondescript metal door, the only interruption in an otherwise unmarked brick façade that ran the length of the block.

"Gimme the cash, I'll come back with the pedal."

George counted out six twenties as the guy turned to me.

"What about you? Gotta be something you need."

Only a year older than me, George prided himself on being a lot more experienced in all the ways that counted: He'd taken me to my first porno movie, gotten me stoned for the first time, and taught me how to crack open the tiny capsules of nitrous oxide used for mixing whipped cream in order to suck out the gas and get high. "Stick with me, Jimmy, and I'll even get you laid!" he vowed.

George trusted the Rush dude, but something about the situation struck me as strange. I pondered the Rototoms, and then I thought about Al Rocky: "I can order anything—an' wit' a big discount!"

"Nah. Nothin'."

The guy jumped out of the car and disappeared through the metal door. After half an hour, George followed and found himself in the employee's break room at the rear of Macy's. He proceeded to scour the first floor of the department store for twenty minutes, and then finally returned to the station wagon.

"What happened?"

"*Coño!* Waddya think?"

He cursed again, shook his head, and made me swear I'd never mention it again.

A few weeks later, I went to call on Al Rocky. I found Giuseppe/Joe sitting in his lawn chair on the sidewalk in front of the now-empty store, smoking a cigarette through his tracheotomy hole. The guy in the black fedora was nowhere to be seen, and neither was Al.

"HAVEN'T. SEEN. YOU. IN. A. WHILE."

I didn't say anything. I knew before he told me.

"AL. DIED."

"When?"

"JUNE."

"I'm sorry."

"HIS. SON. SOLD. DA. PLACE."

I nodded.

"DAMNEDEST. THING."

My first thought was that from now on, I'd be buying my cymbal felts on my own. And then I wondered why I'd never bothered to ask him what was so special about that steak.

Another Day at the Video Store
Kevin Smokler

I'm lucky. When my first book came out, the resulting opportunities meant I didn't have to supplement my writing with a series of retail jobs. I'd worked some kind of counter gig since graduating from college over a decade ago, a proud member of the chronically overqualified. Low stress and not great pay, these half-jobs still kept me in free movies/records/concert tickets/bruised produce and left time to write. But with a book under my belt, an agent wanting another, and the chance to do it full-time and still have weekends off, a babysitting shift at a dusky video store didn't seem worth keeping. Suddenly my time had a value set by something other than opening and closing. Was nine hours worth $50 and waived late fees? I had something called a "career" now. I didn't think I'd miss explaining the difference between Tim Robbins and Tim Allen to insistent housewives all that much.

Or maybe it was just that day that finished me off . . .

The strangest day I ever had working retail occurred a month before I bailed out of counter life forever. I was one of eight clerks at Vault Video in the North Beach neighborhood of San Francisco. Jack Kerouac had roamed these streets as a young man and Lawrence Ferlinghetti still owned City Lights Books a few blocks away. The opening montage of *Dirty Harry* had been filmed in the park across the street. Rumor had it Francis Coppola walked over from his offices down Columbus Avenue and rented movies once in a while. I never saw him.

The rest of the store's clientele mirrored the demographic shifts of the last two decades in the neighborhood: Italian families and their elderly relatives browsed alongside the yuppies who moved in to be near the downtown financial district. About twice a shift, one of the neighborhood homeless folk would stop in and make conversation. Two Feathers, a sleepy-eyed Filipino who slept in the *Dirty Harry* park, would rent two action movies a month, pay in cash, then ask me to hold his booty behind the counter until closing. He never came back for them, never asked for his money back and repeated the whole process a few weeks later. I never figured that out.

Vault Video was flagship of a chain of three stores scattered around the city. Kevin Smith, *Empire Records*, and zines like *Retail Whore* have made it easy to romanticize them as part of dying species: the local video store—with its colorful staff and deep selection, with shelf categories like "Little People and Losers" or "Women Who Kick Ass," being elbowed into oblivion, first by Blockbuster, then Netflix, pay-per-view, and downloading. But I'd worked at enough of these stores to know that was one cliché of many: a well-meaning owner who wanted to be down with the kids, an overly dedicated savant of a manager, a staff with too many opinions and nowhere to put them, and an infrastructure held together by electric tape and computers from 1972. Vault Video may have been "independent," but independent from what? In San Francisco, a solo retail business with loads of personality and crappy facilities was as common as a gay couple holding hands.

For lack of better plans, I had agreed to work a double shift that Saturday, 10 AM to 11 PM on that fateful day. It was sunny and cold, early November. The wind and last night's strong take of returns made it hard to open the front door. All video stores at this level use the same ghetto-ass system to handle after-hours drop-offs: a slot in the door with a cardboard box underneath it. If you had a solid night of returns, the box, weighed down with movies, blocked your way in. We lost hundreds of dollars in merchandise every year to this dumbassery: videotapes that missed the box and cracked open on the floor, or DVDs scuffed when a hungover clerk kicked the box over trying to get inside.

Once in, the first order of business was checking in the returns and getting them back into circulation. I'd been at it maybe ten minutes when the phone rang.

"Vault Video, this is Kevin."

"Hello Kevin, this is Randy McMasters."

Randy McMasters got the job managing Vault because he rented five movies a day for the first six months the store was open. Never missed a day, never had a late fee. He always gave both his first and last name as if I'd never met him and had a habit of asking questions that didn't need answers.

"Just want to go over a few things with you, Kevin, before the day starts. Is that OK?"

What am I going to say? No?

"Are you at the counter?"

No, I'm taking this call from the roof.

"Did you plug in the phone?"

This yellow plastic U I'm talking into? Yes. Yes I did.

"OK, well Kevin Smokler, if you need anything just let me

47

know. And I'll speak to you later. Later in the day. Have a good one."

You too. Now leave me alone.

I'd barely gotten Randy off the phone and returned to the drop-offs when my first customer walked in, a thin, slouching man who looked like he'd just come from fondling a busload of school children. I got the creeps without even looking up at him.

"Hi."

He walked to the center of the store, stopped, and looked back at me. I pretended not to notice.

"Can I ask you something?"

Filing returns. Not looking up. Contemplating making a run for it through the front window.

"Do you have any movies of the adult variety?"

This is a question people only ask when trying to impress you with how open-minded they are. In San Francisco, you can buy porn from a nun. And every video store in America that isn't Blockbuster or located in a church basement carries smut titles. It's how they stayed in business before every perversion this side of gorilla fisting could be satisfied on the Internet. Asking if we carry them is like wearing a sandwich board that says "I watch porn. Yay me!" It's as exhibitionistic as it is unnecessary.

I pointed to our upstairs landing.

"It's my birthday."

What the hell was I supposed to say to that? "Super! I baked you a cake"?

"Happy Birthday."

"I like beautiful asses."

Now I wasn't just scared but angry. I may have been a minimum-wage flunky in this establishment, but until 11 PM it was *my establishment*. And I was not leading off a thirteen-hour day talking beautiful asses with this imbecile.

I left my arm in the air.

"Upstairs. Anything you want."

And with that, he turned around and walked out of the store. Didn't go upstairs, didn't rent anything, didn't look for his beautiful asses. He was a verbal equivalent of a flasher. And when I didn't play along, he went to find some other clerk trapped behind the counter at eleven in the morning.

I went back to the returns, not knowing that was only the beginning.

A few hours passed and the day had settled into its comfortable routine. I'd eaten lunch, watched a movie, and chewed the rag with the midday customers, families mostly and a few couples back from brunch or the gym. Standard stuff, really, until a teal Honda Civic pulled up to our front door, hazard lights blazing. A blond woman in a corduroy jacket and mittens got out and headed for my counter at a dead run.

This is never a good sign. A significant percentage of weekday rentals are spontaneous: The renter is headed home from work but upon passing the store decides, "Hey, a movie might be nice." Since their mind is already at home on their couch, these customers are often curt and rude, seeing any pleasantry as an obstacle to their eminent relaxation.

The weekend versions of this customer are the worst. Not only is their hurry rude, but, since it's the weekend and they're not members of the clergy, usually pointless too.

Corduroy Jacket charged through my front door and stopped about five feet in. Pointing a finger at my head, she yelled out a single word . . .

"*Gladiator!*"

Video-store clerks dream about these moments. Customers who get intimidated by browsing will stand in the center of the store calling out movie names. Not "Excuse me? Could you help me find *Star Wars*?" but "*Star Wars? Star Wars?*" as if the movie will appear from behind a corner and leap into their lap. This is the video business equivalent of *Are You My Mother?*, which has not seemed to carry over to other businesses. (Do you go the post office and yell out "Stamps!" to no one in particular?) As such, clerks spend hours coming up with smart-ass answers to these inquiries. A man once came in and shouted "*A Few Good Men!*" at me. I answered "Why? Am I not enough for you?"

I was in a good mood and didn't want to insult her. So I let her dangle.

"Come again?"

"Do you have the movie *Gladiator*?"

I fetched it and keyed her account into the computer. She had $183 in late fees.

"Ma'am, you have $183 in late fees. I can't rent to you with this much money outstanding."

She looked at me. I pointed to the screen.

"Can I use your phone?"

I handed her the phone.

"Hi Jim? It's Kate . . . Yes, I'm at the video store. They say we owe $183 in late fees and I know this isn't for my movies . . . I don't care if we're getting divorced, I didn't run up these late fees . . . Well I'm calling my attorney as soon as I get home and these are going right on the settlement."

And with that, she slammed down the phone and flew into her waiting Civic, lights still blinking.

Fifteen minutes later, another car pulled up, same hurry, same hazard lights. A tall man in a fleece windbreaker strode in.

"My name's Jim."

Of course it is.

"Hi Jim."

"Did my wife just leave here saying I owed you guys $183 in late fees?"

"Yes she did."

"Well she's lying."

"Don't know what to tell you, Jim. I can't rent on an account with $183 in late fees."

And with that, he slammed a credit card on the counter.

"Tell that bitch I'll see her in court!"

Randy called an hour later to get a midday report. I told him we'd just covered payroll for the entire weekend on the collapse of the Tomlinson marriage and that the store may be called as a material witness should it go to court. As least that's what Jim said before he left.

Good times.

By late that evening, my friend Laura had come down to the store to hang out. We each worked a few weekend days a month and kept each other company on those nights, arguing about movies (she liked morbid dramas; I preferred what she called "comedies about young attractive people trying to find love in the 1990s") and razzing our favorite customers. I loved those evenings. Laura and I are still friends.

Come 11 PM though, and the bar was closed. No matter how much fun we were having, thirteen hours was more than enough of this business. Sign on the door said we close at eleven, and we close at eleven. At eleven, Laura locked the front door and flipped the sign over to CLOSED. I began powering down the computer and scrubbing the day's gunk off the counter. Ten minutes into cleanup and there was a knock on the door.

"We're closed!" Laura and I called out.

Pause. The knockers, a couple in expensive leather jackets, weren't moving. We kept cleaning up.

"Please?"

"We're closed. Come back tomorrow."

I heard dejected footsteps head off down the block. I heard the same footsteps come back. A manicured hand reached into the return slot holding what looked like a valet parking ticket.

"Not even for ten dollars?"

Now I was mad. I just spent thirteen hours on my feet. I had to discuss pornography with a disciple of the Zodiac Killer and was in the crossfire of a crumbling marriage. I had a master's degree and clips at national magazines and newspapers and my manager still thought I was an idiot. I may have made $7 an hour but my escape would not be bought off for the cost of a pan pizza. *Read the fucking sign. I have a personal life too.*

I looked at Laura, who was practically spitting fire. It took us three seconds to answer.

"Not even for ten dollars!"

Ms. Ten Dollars and her friends suck off down Union Street. Laura opened the door and flipped them off. Even though they didn't turn around, we exploded laughing.

After helping me restock the shelves, Laura said goodnight and headed home. I walked to the back of the store to turn the main lights off when the phone rang.

"Hi Kevin, this is Randy McMasters. Still at the store?"

I'm not answering that.

"How did it go today?"

Even now, nearly six years later, I don't know what happened in that moment. I'd never confided in Randy, didn't ever think much about him when I wasn't working. But before I could stop myself, I told him the whole story of everything that happened that day, pacing about the empty, locked store with the street awakening to the late night outside.

It took about a half hour of arm waving and exasperation to get the whole thing out. Our voices tired from the laughing, Randy spoke. It was the one time I'd heard him say something that wasn't air filler but both obvious and exactly right.

"Well Kevin," he said. "Sounds like just another day at the video store."

Not Included with Display
Michael Beaumier

It's been my experience that people don't have the slightest idea what they want, and will stop at nothing to get it. They will over-pay for ugly shoes they will never wear, stand in line to buy tacky clothes they don't really like, and riot the morning after Thanksgiving for the honor of being among the first into Wal-Mart. People don't know what they want, so they buy anything, everything—as if they have a craving for some kind of food but they're not sure what, so they eat whatever is put in front of them, even if they aren't really hungry.

It is also been my experience that people do not appreciate having such things pointed out to them while they're shopping, so I keep my mouth shut. I work in one of those big department stores, in what they call the "home department" specifically, I sell stuff for the kitchen. The shelves and tables around me are filled with odd little devices, doodads, and tools that are sup-posed to help the average person master the art of preparing food, but I can't say I honestly believe this, and I'm not just say-ing that because I hate to cook. But it seems as if how the mer-chandise is displayed counts more than what the merchandise actually *is*. A lot of effort goes into arranging and lighting this stuff—the melon-ball-fork sharpeners, the stainless-steel bacon frothers, the latex egg coasters offered in an assortment of shocking pastel hues—and despite the fact that most of these things are useless, if not ridiculous, the results can be summed up in two words: *utterly irresistible*.

"How much are those pans?" a woman asked me. "They're gorgeous!" Her eyes were almost dancing in her head, reflecting the glossy light that had been placed, just so, to show the eight-piece set of copper pots and skillets to their utmost advantage.

The price didn't faze her in the least; she simply had to have them. Besides, she told me, she read something once about how aluminum pans cause Alzheimer's—so this would be, *medicinally*, a wise purchase.

"Well," I told her, "you should probably know these pans have aluminum in them, too. There's anodized aluminum in the—"

"I don't care," she snapped. Her credit card was already out, and nothing was going to make her lose her shopping buzz. "It's anodized aluminum, which I'm sure is much safer, right? Can you have these delivered?"

It was like that a lot, in a variety of ways. There was a woman who purchased three different sizes of the exact same food processor—the pro-chef, the home, and the mini—because, as she said, "you never know," and the man who purchased eighty carbon-steel knives for reasons I thought best not to inquire after. There are people I saw nearly every day who purchased whatever cookware, bakeware, silverware, device, or tool that struck their fancy, and they often bought in quantity. No one really needs even one citrus peeler; how, then, to explain anyone who'd purchase four or five at a time?

"It's a fetish," Adam the display manager once told me.

"People just can't help themselves." Adam was the guy in charge of arranging, lighting, and positioning all the merchandise in the department, and he very rarely spoke to anyone. He was not the friendliest fellow you'll ever encounter, but I was asking, which he seemed to feel was an opportunity to put me in my place. The display people regarded themselves as the backbone of the store, and to be honest, their constant arrogance wasn't without reason. Adam could set up a display of toothpicks and used Kleenex in the morning, and we'd have been sold out by midafternoon.

"It's not like how it works in clothes, or shoes, or luggage, or any of the other departments," Adam drawled, his voice filled with exasperation. When Adam talked, he talked with his hands, slow languid movements that matched his voice, expressing his complete boredom at having to stoop to talk to you at all. "Though shoes comes closest. With this kitchen stuff, people just want it—want, want, *want*, no matter what it does, or how expensive it is. Frankly, dear," he addressed me without eye contact, "you're really quite *superfluous* to the entire equation, *n'est pas?* These things, they practically sell themselves—at least, after I work my magic on them."

I started to protest, but Adam merely raised one hand and instantly silenced me.

"It's not about *you*," he told me. "It's about the *merchandise*." And although he was the one who walked away, it felt as if I was the one who'd been dismissed.

I couldn't help but get progressively more depressed after that. A man is supposed to have value and substance, isn't he? A man is not supposed to compare himself to a bunch of steamers and Crock-Pots and waffle irons and come up short, or be invisible compared to sterling silver corkscrews.

It wasn't long before I began to act out. Glasses and dishes began to show telltale smudges, as if someone—some crazed person, I'm sure, with extremely dirty hands—had intentionally left fingerprints everywhere. Lights were moved, or their bulbs unscrewed and left dark, and the kitchen devices, suddenly thrown into shadow, became less items to be coveted than implements of danger and menace.

"I don't know about that espresso maker," I told one prospective shopper as I ran my fingers across the dials and buttons. "You see this here? This red light? That tells you when the pressure's gotten too high. I tell you, if you see that light, you better run." I plugged the machine in, and in the darkness the red light sprang to life instantaneously. I turned around, and the customer was nowhere to be seen.

I loved it.

They fired me.

No Good Deed . . .
Anita Liberty

It wasn't my fault. It was theirs. They never should have trusted me. They knew I had been recently dumped. They had my full disclosure. I was in the midst of experiencing some serious PTSD (post-traumatic stress disorder). I shouldn't have been making any big decisions, operating heavy machinery, or watching my friends' high-end gift store in Los Angeles for two days while they went to a trade show in San Francisco.

I had settled myself in Los Angeles for a couple of months in the hopes of furthering my career; in finding success, I hoped to humiliate my ex-boyfriend, Mitchell, to get even with him for dumping me for a woman named Heather. I had steadily been building an audience on the East Coast through live performances in New York City and felt ready to move on to a bigger pond. I was also hoping—given the predominant interests of most of the people who live out there—that these Los Angeles shows might even allow me the opportunity to infiltrate other media, such as film and television. I put the word out to friends that I was interested in performing and needed a venue. A friend of mine mentioned some people he knew who had recently opened a store in West Hollywood called Zipper. He urged me to meet the proprietors, Steven and Elizabeth. He told me that they were interested in having their gift store be *more* than just a gift store. Steven and Elizabeth wanted to showcase artists' work on their walls and host performances and readings. I thought it might be cool to perform in a store. I've always loved the feeling of being in a store at night. It makes shopping seem so much more like entertainment and so much less like buying a bunch of stuff you don't need and can't really afford just 'cause you're desperately trying to fill the gaping hole left by your boyfriend of three and a half years when he yanked out your still-beating heart and stepped on it on his way out the door to meet up with his new girlfriend.

I loved Steven and Elizabeth immediately. They were warm and welcoming and I wanted them to like me. In fact, I recall telling them at our first meeting that my "friend garage" was nearing capacity, but if they moved fast enough and were willing to drop into an Indiana-Jones-type roll before the door slammed shut to the ground, they could make it in and be in there for life. They said they'd think about it. I told them they didn't have much time. I liked them as people, it's true, but I also liked the idea of being friends with storeowners. It seemed like that would truly be a friendship with *benefits*. I imagined it would sort of be the equivalent of being friends with a bartender if you were an alcoholic. I've never been much of a drinker, but I do like to shop. And I love getting things for free. Or at least at a deep discount. I also quite enjoyed the thought that I would always know where they were between certain hours on certain days and that I could feel free to drop in on them spontaneously at any time during those hours and they'd have to acknowledge me. Not only that, they'd have to be *nice* to me, 'cause I was never going to be just a friend to them. As long as I had a valid credit card, I was a potential customer. It gave me a sense of security I hadn't known before in a relationship. They would always be there and they would always be at my mercy. It was comforting.

At any rate, on the professional side, we set up some dates for me to perform. The shows went fine. They were well attended and the novelty of seeing a performance in a store worked to all of our advantages. People who came to see me, but who hadn't been to the store before, were delighted to discover it, and Zipper's regular customers were excited to be there after hours and be part of some sort of *happening*. It felt good to be onstage (or, rather, on the plastic milk crate I had to stand on in order for everyone to see me since I'm short and was performing in a store instead of on a real stage). On the personal side, my friendship with Steven and Elizabeth was coming along nicely. After the shows were over, I still had a few weeks left in Los Angeles. Without much to do, I'd end up going over to Zipper just to hang out. We'd order in lunch and sit on the floor and eat it while we waited for customers. I felt like part of the team. So when Steven and Elizabeth asked me if I'd be interested in watching the store for them for the weekend they were to be in San Francisco, I didn't hesitate. They needed me and I was at a point in my life where I needed to feel needed.

Besides, how hard could it be to store-sit? It was like house-sitting. Well, except for the fact that complete strangers would be coming through my friends' "house" and touching all my friends' things. But I, too, would be able to touch all their things—wantonly, frequently, without the pretense of deciding whether to buy anything. I could wear the jewelry. I could read the glossy design books. I could sit on the grey velvet couch and lean against the blue-sequined cushions. I would do what all house sitters do: I would pretend it was my home.

The day before Steven and Elizabeth were to leave, they walked me through my responsibilities. They showed me what I needed to do to open the store in the morning and how to close the store in the evening. There were several things that they specifically called to my attention. One was that I needed to remove an antique wall sconce before I pulled the internal gate shut. OK. No biggie. The other was that I should be aware of shoplifters. Umm . . . duh! And that I should be nice to the customers no matter what. That felt like the one direction that was gonna be the hardest to follow. *No matter what?* I have trouble being nice under the *best* of circumstances. Besides, being a shopper myself, I know what it's like to walk randomly in and out of stores lost in my own thoughts, carrying my own feelings around, engaged in an internal struggle that becomes external the minute some chipper young thing asks me if I need any help. For the most part, I really don't like people who work in retail. I don't want them to help me. I don't want them to follow me around, help me make decisions, put things back in place the minute I've nudged them out. But here I was, in the position of running my own store. I was going to have to wait on people. And I was going to have to pretend to care. I was going to have to act the part. And I'm a terrible actress. But I knew I couldn't just alienate Zipper's customers willy-nilly. That wouldn't be fair to Steven and Elizabeth. They had built and nurtured and grown their business. It was their baby. I had effectively agreed to babysit and I wasn't just gonna let the kid starve.

My first morning felt pretty exciting. I had the keys to my

very own store. It was like being a kid in a candy store. Or a struggling performance poet in a high-end gift store. It was fun. I came in the back. I turned on the lights as directed. I removed the antique wall sconce before opening the interior gate and then replaced it once the gate was pulled back. It was a beautiful sunny day. It was Los Angeles. I had a function, a purpose. I was gonna sell stuff. I had nowhere to be but here for the next eight hours. It felt oddly liberating, except for the fact that I couldn't actually go anywhere. I did have one of those signs available to me that storekeepers tape to the door that say: *Back in a few minutes*. And we all know that that means that the shopkeeper had to go to the bathroom. As a shopper, I always feel awkward waiting around for that person to return. Besides the fact that sometimes five minutes isn't five minutes at all. But if I had to go, I'd have to go.

I unlocked the front door and immediately felt conflicted about my expectations. I wanted customers to stream through the store needing and wanting and buying so I could prove to Steven and Elizabeth (and myself) that I could interact with the common man and seduce him into pulling out his credit card and purchasing something expensive on impulse. On the other hand, I liked being by myself surrounded by beautiful things and didn't really want any random strangers coming in and disturbing my fantasy life. I walked around the store, pretending to straighten displays, realign edges, fluff pillows.

But really I was just staking out my territory. This was my store now. This was my home. I lived in a place with a lot of handblown vases and artsy coasters and almond soap and lacquered boxes and all the Coke I could drink (Steven and Elizabeth were addicts and kept their mini-fridge stocked). The steady supply of Coke was particularly important as I was in a low-grade depression and had been taking a lot of naps. I would need some extra support around 3:30 PM or so when the novelty of being a storeowner wore off and my cheeseburger and fries started sucking the blood from my brain and I remembered that I was miserable and lonely and frustrated. But the need for artificial stimulants was hours off and for the moment I was on a natural high as I stood behind the counter and lovingly fondled each and every expensive piece of jewelry as if it were my own. I caressed them.

I wore them. They belonged to me. After all, they were in *my* store.

It was a pretty slow morning at my store. I should mention, for the record and for the sake of clarity, that it was January. January is notoriously the worst month for retail. Everyone has already kind of shot his or her wad, both in financial terms and giddy enthusiastic shopping terms, during the December holidays. Steven and Elizabeth had prepared me that customers might be few and far between. Maybe that's why they were so willing to leave a retail novice like me in charge.

Before I could sink into any kind of despair or figure out how to nap standing up with my eyes open, I heard the door. A customer!! My first customer. And it was a boy! Well, technically, a man. And he was adorable. (To be honest, I really have no recollection what the hell he looked like, but my story works a lot better if he's at least attractive, so allow me some artistic license here.) I would have no problem nurturing this customer. We would talk and laugh and flirt and sell and buy and let our hands touch *by mistake* as he handed me his Platinum American Express card for the aqua suede ottoman and the chocolate alpaca throw, which he would buy purely on my recommendation because he wants to impress women with his good taste and I'm exactly the kind of woman he wants to impress. He smiled at me and walked past the counter. I smiled back.

"Let me know if you need anything," I called after him as he made his way to the back of the store.

"I will," he called back cheerfully.

I stood straighter. I tried to look official, without seeming too rigid. I had a lot going on. In a few painful minutes, he returned to where I stood at the counter with a greeting card in his hands. He handed it to me. I felt disappointed. "That's it? A fucking card?" I wanted to yell. But I didn't, because that would have been bad. Instead, I smiled and rang it up. I gave him his total and he handed me a couple bucks. At the last minute, he said, "Wait, I think I have change." He pulled some change from his pocket and it fell clumsily from his fingers to the counter. A couple of quarters rolled off my side of the counter onto the floor. I bent down to get them. I stood up and handed them to him. He thanked me and then he twinkled at me. I swear he did. He *twinkled*. I forgave him his limited impulse-buying budget and he gave me exact change. He took his card, waved good-bye, and left.

I felt pretty proud of myself. It wasn't a big moment, but my ego was so in need of being stroked that I turned the sale of a greeting card into a personal accomplishment. I stood there spinning thoughts about my future in retail and how I'd eventually open my own store and stock it with Anita Liberty merchandise—*i hate him* T-shirts and *i'm not bitter* mugs and *not thinking about you* thongs—and then I realized that an extremely cool calculator that had been displayed on the counter was *gone*.

It had been there a minute ago and now it was gone. It was a clear plastic calculator that rolled into a tube. It was cool and it was there and now it wasn't. The display calculator was missing as well as the one that had been next to it still in its box. I checked everywhere on the counter. I looked on the floor, behind the cash box, under wrapping paper. It wasn't there. That twinkly guy stole it! He twinkled at me and then stole something from me. He twinkled at me just *so* he could steal something from me. It was that damned twinkle. It'd been so long since some guy twinkled at me that I got taken by surprise. It was like shining a bright light in the eyes of a deer. I froze. Bastard. Twinkly-eyed bastard. I felt terrible. I had failed Steven and Elizabeth. And, beyond that, I felt so *violated*. I had dropped my guard for one second, *one second*, and I paid a price. I wasn't sure of the exact price, but if I had a *calculator*, maybe I'd have been able to figure it out.

The rest of the day was relatively uneventful. I watched everyone like a hawk and was sure not to let anyone look at me in any way that felt overly friendly or distracting. I was glad when the day was over and I could lock up. I closed out the cash register, settled up the credit card receipts, blew out the candles, turned off the lights, and went to pull the interior gate shut. It was stuck, so I pulled it harder. It wasn't budging. I really yanked on it. And then I heard the crunching of metal. The wall sconce. Right. Forgot about that. I released my hold on the gate and went to survey the damage. A crumpled piece of metal hung where the antique wall sconce had been just a moment ago. I carefully took it down, pulled the gate shut, returned the hunk o' metal to its hook and called it a day.

When Steven and Elizabeth returned, I gave them the

breakdown. Basically, I sold very little, a couple of calculators got stolen, I broke an irreplaceable wall sconce, and I don't know, but it's possible that I alienated some people. But that just comes under the *collateral damage* heading. They had to expect some customers to fall. As I said before, it was their fault for trusting me in the first place. We had never discussed any type of compensation for my stepping in and helping them out, so I told them that I'd just take the clear glass bracelet I'd been coveting and we'd consider ourselves even.

They looked at me, but they didn't protest. Or at least not quickly enough, so I slipped the bracelet on and told them to call me if they ever needed me again.

Steven and Elizabeth and I have remained close friends. Our friendship is a lot stronger than two groovy calculators, a wall sconce, and a one-of-a-kind bracelet. I mean, it's not like I lost them a *huge* amount of money. It's not like they came to visit me at my happenin' new Brooklyn apartment one day years later and we walked around the neighborhood and I strongly encouraged them to consider opening a store a block and a half away from my apartment 'cause I told them how much people *love* to shop in Brooklyn and how much *disposable income* the residents have and how *cool* it would be to have a store on both coasts. It's not like they actually opened that store and it became such a source of personal inconvenience and distress and irritation that they ended up deciding to close it. It's not like I forced them into that kind of situation or anything. That would have been really bad.

(N.B.: For the four years that the Brooklyn branch of Zipper was open, Steven and Elizabeth never asked me to watch the store for them . . . not once. Not when their store manager was

67

out sick and both of them were stuck in Los Angeles, not if something came up at the last minute, not if they wanted to go out for lunch, not if they had to go to the bathroom, not if they were in a real bind and were discussing openly—*while I was standing right there*—what they were going to do with the store and how would they ever find anyone on such short notice. But I've chosen not to take that personally. They're in my friend garage and I'm not letting them out—no matter how many times they ask—because as long as they're in there I know I can get a discount at Zipper.)

We Weren't Really Rock Stars
Richard Cox

Like anyone, I believe my expectations to be reasonable.

When I walk into a store that sells electronics, for instance, I don't expect any of the clerks to know anything. In fact, I would prefer it if they chose not to acknowledge my presence at all. I would rather wander through the rows of televisions and stereos and computers at my own pace, Internet research in hand, maybe turn a knob here and there, run my fingers along the smooth geometrical shapes of technology.

But here you come, Mr. Sales Clerk. You in your pleated tan pants, your wrinkled Oxford, in your necktie of many colors. Here you come to interrupt my joy with your offer to "help" me. Your name is John. Your eyes shimmer with boredom, your breath reeks of Krispy Kreme. Exactly how do you propose to "help" me?

Look, John. I know what it's like to stand in the stockroom and make fun of stupid customers. I've already been excited by that $20 bonus on Motorola phones. I've been forced to sell extended warranties, which you and I both know are pure profit for the retail giant and a complete waste of money for me, the customer.

I know all this, John, because I used to be a sales clerk just like you.

Yes, I sold televisions and stereos and computers. I even sold mobile phones, except in my day most of them came in bags, and the portable versions were the size of residential bricks.

My years in retail were shaped by a strong work ethic and intense apathy for customers. The work ethic came by way of my father, who convinced me as a youngster that if I couldn't outsmart someone, or outmaneuver them, I could always outwork them. He's a product of the postwar generation, my dad is, and he embodied the concept of "Git-R-Done" long before faux-redneck comedian Larry the Cable Guy stumbled across the term while trying on another of his custom-made, no-sleeve flannel shirts.

My apathy, meanwhile, grew out of the retail experience itself.

So listen up, Johnny Sales Clerk: I may not need your help, but I will never be rude to you, because I know how it feels to be accosted by unreasonable customers. I know the oppression of inept management. And if you want to survive your man-made Hell, if you choose to roam the fluorescent aisles with a smile, I can tell you how to do it.

Make a friend.

I stalked my retail job. Longed for it. At nineteen years old, the concept of being paid for performance was unheard of, and stories of sales associates earning $400 or $500 a week in commission made me salivate like a dog. I was making $100 a week. I toiled deep in the stock room, inside an office made of plywood, evaluating unwanted merchandise generated by our no-hassle return policy. It was work a monkey could have been trained to do.

So when I heard our store planned to expand its electronics department, I pulled every string I could think of to land myself an interview. The store manager was only vaguely impressed with me, but I also befriended the senior sales associate, a man with twenty-five years of experience with the company. He could see a bit of my dad in me, I think, and I was pretty much a lock to land the position. Then I walked out onto the sales floor one day and saw a new face staring back at me. A short fellow in a plaid shirt and a sock tie.

"Who are you?" I asked this stranger.

"Who are *you*?" he asked me back.

Thus began my long friendship with a fellow named Brian.

It turned out the electronics department wanted to add *two* new sales associates, and Brian was hired few weeks before me. I was insanely jealous of him, of his easy camaraderie with the other associates already on the team. We were both new, but it was me on the bottom of the schedule, not him.

Ours was a department store, so electronics was one of only several sales groups. The furniture team made decent money, but the product was boring. The guys over in lawn and garden wore red vests and weren't really taken seriously. Appliances were our company's most popular products, and you could make good money in that department, but the most glamorous team in the entire store was us. In electronics, we were rock stars.

And why not? We were paid to stand around and watch television all day. To play with video cameras. If a customer wanted to hear a pair of $800 speakers, we demonstrated them with our favorite music. We were college students in a college town, and young women shopped in the store all the time. When they needed a new VCR, they came to us.

One thing you should know about service agreements and

extended warranties—don't ever buy them. Our company expected these warranties to comprise 10 percent of our gross sales because it made so much money on them. Here's why: If a piece of electronic equipment doesn't break down in the first few weeks, it will usually operate for years with no problem. And since early failures are usually covered by the product's standard warranty, any extra coverage you pay for is a gamble you will almost always lose.

I could never get past the reality of this, so I was horrible at selling service agreements. Brian, however, was a master at it. Not because he was a good liar, but because he managed to convince himself they were a good deal. And if you actually brought your VCR in for a professional cleaning every year, perhaps they were.

In fact, Brian became so adept at selling these agreements that he ranked near the top among all sales associates in the entire country—which was no small feat at a company that boasted more than a thousand full-line stores. He was a star among stars . . . at least until the day one of his customers called the store to complain about a big-screen TV. It was standard fare, a perfect example of extended warranty coverage, but somehow our company found a loophole in the contract and denied coverage. Brian was furious—so angry, in fact, that he stopped selling service agreements altogether. Even when customers inquired about them (oh, how trained they were), Brian would talk them out of it.

The two of us talked at length about how Brian could be fired for such insubordination, so I helped him draft a letter that he mailed to various managers up the retail food chain. Neither of us expected much to come of it, so you can imagine our surprise on the day the president of our company called the store, apology ready. Mr. Big Time not only arranged service for the TV, but he also asked Brian to reconsider his position on the warranties. We were astonished. And further emboldened.

Rock stars, indeed.

It would be mistake to portray Brian and I as saints—nothing could be further from the truth. Not when our favorite game was to try and make each other laugh while we waited on customers. One evening I heard Brian fielding questions from a woman with an unusual accent, so I did what any responsible sales associate might do—I walked up behind her and made faces at him. Brian caved, cracked a smile, and the woman turned quickly around. She accused me of doing exactly what I was doing, and I denied it—innocently, of course—but the woman would have none of it. She marched away, toward the customer service desk, and for a moment I thought my career in that store was over. But then I remembered—I was a sales associate in electronics, for Pete's sake! I darted into the stockroom, sprinting through the heart of the store while the woman circled its perimeter, and located the on-duty manager. I explained how the woman had misunderstood something I said—a preemptive strike—and the manager smiled warmly at me. Told me not to worry about some silly customer.

My skin may as well have been made of Teflon.

Sales were good, and as the months wore on, Brian and I grew bolder. Even the hiring of a sweet but in-over-her-head sales manager couldn't deter us. This woman was responsible for both appliances and electronics, but since she didn't know much about our products, she mainly left us alone.

One night Brian and I were working on a sales display after the store had closed. The manager on duty saw us during her last-minute walk-through and asked us to finish up, but we ignored her. And then lost track of time, of course. By the time we made it to the back door, expecting the on-duty manager to be waiting for us, everyone was gone. The store was locked, and we couldn't get out.

Remember, this was a major department store chain. A thousand full-line stores and even more specialty locations. The stores were monitored during the day by local loss prevention associates and after hours by a centralized security firm. Brian and I didn't know anything about the late-night security, however. We also didn't know the phone number of the on-duty manager, and our own manager didn't pick up when we called her.

We were stuck.

But did we go back to our department and watch television? Find a place to sleep in the furniture department?

Nah. We picked out a couple of bicycles and raced each other around the store. As fast as we could. Neither one of us realized it, but we left long streaks of rubber all over the store. We also had no idea we were setting off motion detectors in rapid succession, something that caught the amused attention of the remote security firm. It wasn't long before the store manager showed up, and then the on-duty manager, and then our own manager. By then Brian and I were waiting innocently at the back door, sweating and out of breath. "We were working so hard on that display," the two of us explained, "that we forgot what time it was."

Everyone laughed.

74

When you're paid on commission, it's easy to steer customers toward the product that will make you the most money. Even among products that are priced the same, the commission percentage is often different. Brian and I tried hard not to sell junk to customers, even when it meant a few extra bucks on our checks, but not all of our teammates agreed with us. What surprised me the most was how much money some of the other sales clerks earned considering their limited knowledge of the products. One year, when the holidays arrived, Brian and I bought the worst offender a children's book that explained electronics in a rudimentary way. It was funny, to be sure, but every month that ignorant guy laughed all the way to the bank.

Brian left the store a year before I did, and things weren't quite as fun after that. Our manager became a little more involved with electronics as the company tried to compete against specialty stores like Best Buy and Circuit City. We had long suspected she was having an affair with a married fellow over in appliances, and a few months after I quit, the two lovers were fired. Turns out they had been embezzling money for months.

I've been friends with Brian for seventeen years. He lives in California now, and I live in Oklahoma. We see each other twice a year, usually to play golf. Last year I nominated him for the World's Worst Swing, a contest sponsored by *Golf Digest* and The Golf Channel. I put together a funny video of his worst shots, and a few months later the footage appeared on national television. Guess who won the contest? So OK, Brian: You sold more service agreements than me, but at least I don't have the world's worst golf swing.

Every so often I return to visit my alma mater, and while there I always stop by the store. The sales associates don't wear plaid shirts anymore, they don't wear sock ties, but really the clothes aren't much better. And as you might expect, I invariably see a few clerks standing around, watching television.

In fact, here comes one of them now. Hands shoved in his pockets, eyes darting past me as a cute coed walks by. I'm looking at one of the big screen TVs, stunned at how poorly the picture is calibrated. But should I expect anything else? From what I understand, the clerks aren't paid commission anymore.

Like I said before, I'm reasonable.

"Anything I can help you with, sir?" the clerk asks me.

I look at his badge.

His name is John.

He's not a rock star, but he is me.

He's who I was. Who we were.

Brian and I were just kids, after all, sandwiched between out-of-touch management and a shrinking customer base. We thought we owned the world, and we couldn't have been more wrong.

But we did have each other.

And we still do.

Other Things in Mind
James Wagner

I was helping a rich woman from the wealthy suburbs. She was trying to buy a water heater. She was in her early seventies, gilded, with weekly hair-appointment hair, expensive sweatpants, and serious jewelry (weaponry?). She continued to ask and re-ask questions. It was a Saturday. I had a lot to do.

"There are so many choices!" she said.

As she was deliberating, I received a phone call, and I took it. I walked a short way away from her, maybe five to ten feet, and saw a middle-aged couple trying to get my attention while I was already talking on the phone. This is common practice by our shoppers. They know you are on the phone with someone, as you are talking right into the phone near them, but they continue to begin asking questions. I have to inevitably hold up a finger to tell them I will be right with them. This will usually work, but many times they persist, as in, "I put a hole in my drywall, and I need to fix it, can you help me with that?"

I turned away from the couple, however, without making eye contact—sometimes I just want to hide in plain sight—and without holding up my "just a minute" finger. As I sensed the phone call was ending, I began walking back to the rich woman who was reviewing the water heater inventory form, which lists dimensions and prices. But I was still on the phone, ending the conversation, when I heard whispers from the couple just behind me—"Sir, sir"—that I continued to ignore. As I said good-bye to the man on the phone, the rich woman, hearing the "Sir, sir," turned around toward me in an aghast, casually uptight way—and upbraided me by telling me, "I am not a 'Sir,' I am a lady." I was confused, initially, by her comment, but then I realized she had mistakenly thought that I had said "Sir, sir" o her, when it was the couple behind me who had said it to me.

I said to the rich woman, "I didn't say that—they did." The couple was now at my side. The female of the couple said, immediately, in shock, "We never said anything of the sort." She was indignant, and the man uttered or did something nonverbally to concur. I turned around and saw what I had already known. We four were the only four in the aisle.

I looked at the couple with an irritated, contorted face, as in, "What are you talking about?" But they ignored my look and my following comments, and they stood, waiting, in assured silence, for me to finish with the rich woman.

About a month or so into my job in the plumbing department, I received a phone call late one night. A young man was on the phone. He asked if we sold any hot water heaters.

I told him we did.

He then asked me if I would mind going over to the aisle where the hot water heaters are, as he had a couple more questions. I could hear some general murmuring in the background. When near the hot water heaters, I asked him what his questions were. He said he just had one now, actually.

"OK," I said, "What is it?"

He asked me if I would look on the boxes of the hot water heaters and see if they said HOT WATER HEATER on them. I heard some laughter in the background.

I earnestly searched for what he was asking for, and then told him, "No, all they say are either GAS WATER HEATER or ELECTRIC WATER HEATER."

"Yeah, that's what I thought," the man said. I could hear one of his friends in the background say, "Ask him why he wants to heat hot water!" before bursting out in laughter.

"Is that it?" I asked.

"Oh, yes, that's it," he said smugly. "Thank you for your help."

Abuse by customers and desired violence toward them by colleagues often go hand in hand, and one of the principle activities of my colleagues at the hardware store is to think of ways of killing customers.

There are the typical, physical interests in choking a customer to death—the underlying incentive seems to be to stop them from speaking anymore.

I've heard colleagues say they wanted to hit some irritating customer with a hammer, a steel pipe, and a toilet.

I've heard another one say he thought of dropping, from twenty feet up, a box of heavy, orange emergency cones on their heads.

But these are really pedestrian remarks made by newer associates who haven't had years of abuse build up in them like the veteran associates have. The veteran associates have more elaborate and extensive plans for killing. They have vision.

One associate, Tom, has imagined—he hasn't figured this out completely yet—somehow draining the water out of the sprinkler system above the store, and supplying the lines with propane gas instead. He would then wait until the store was at its busiest, then he would release the gas from the sprinklers. People, he felt, would swoon, clutching for their throats (see the desire to choke customers, above) and drop in the aisles from inhaling the gas. He would then, as he was walking out the door, throw a match into the building, and the entire store would burn. From a deli across the street, he would watch the store burn, the fire trucks arrive, and the panic.

One day I was walking back toward receiving, and I overheard a short conversation between a middle-aged couple and two associates from electrical. The couple was asking for some item the two electrical associates hadn't heard of, and the associates tried to guess where in the store it might be. The woman was the one interested in having the item.

Frustrated, she then cut off the conversation and said to the associates, "Well, you really are clueless, aren't you?" And then she turned her cart, and began walking toward the area the electrical associates said the item might be.

The supervisor in electrical was one of these associates, and he muttered under his breath toward the other electrical associate, "I guess I am clueless." The other associate mockingly pronounced, "Me too."

I can never really get it out of my head that these comments are oftentimes made by people who are fifty or sixty years old. These are not comments made by teenagers or babies.

The sarcastic comments made by the electrical associates point toward the ridiculous expectations customers sometimes have about the knowledge of items in the store.

When I couldn't figure out where his odd item might be, a customer said to me, "Maybe you should spend some time in the store." I looked at him, feeling the need to choke him, and said, "Well, sir, there are only fifty thousand items in the store, and new items arriving daily. You are asking for something that might be in the area for building. I work in plumbing, and I work part-time."

He walked off.

I've noticed that many customers are shocked to hear that you might have feelings, and that you are a real person apart from your function as an associate. They are so used to treating you like furniture that it is difficult for them when the furniture talks back to them. Something seems upset in the universe. There are pauses and silences and facial reconfigurations by customers before they nearly back away from you, fearful that *all of them*, all of these people working, might actually be people too.

One colleague feels that the failed system of customer-associate interaction is based on a theory he likes to call reverse parenting (he may mean negative reinforcement). The theory follows from the "customer is always right" theory, a theory drummed up by an owner who didn't have to deal with the day-to-day public, who only had to take in their money and then spend it on cars, stocks, and vacations, the likes of which the people who did deal with the public would never see.

Reverse parenting really explains the consequences of a policy like "the customer is always right." It is well known to the public, and it is used daily. It rewards people who raise enough of a ruckus about something, no matter how asinine they are, who ask for extra favors, who *expect* extra favors, at almost every turn. When they don't get their way, my colleague explained, they resort to babylike behavior, throwing fits. And then the company congratulates the fit-throwing by doing anything in its power to calm the infant-customer down, until they are satisfied. The adult customer, like the infant baby, soon learns that if he or she cries enough, he or she will get what he or she wants.

And the specific demands grow more ridiculous with each day I'm at the store. Here's just one example:

In plumbing we sell PVC pipe in eight different diameter sizes, from one-half-inch- to four-inch-diameter pipe. We do not sell PVC pipe by the foot, only by the stick, or the entire ten-foot length. As a side service, we will saw the pipe in half, by hand, so the customers can fit it in their cars. The larger the diameter of the pipe, obviously, the more time and energy is needed to cut the pipe. Not to mention sweat. Cutting a four-inch pipe in half once, by hand, is not digging a ditch, certainly, but it is also not something you want to do too much, as it takes some doing to get through it with the saw.

One day a strong-looking woman came in. She was young and healthy, and she came up to me to tell me she was going to be buying four-inch PVC pipe. I said, "OK." She then asked if I could cut it for her. I told her that I would cut it in half for her, if she needed to get it into her car. She said that wasn't what she had in mind. She had a project. When she said "project," I knew I was going to be in for a bad one. Apart from the weird enthusiasm the customers expect you will share with them, projects always take forever for an associate because many times the customer hasn't thought anything through, including measurements. I kid you not.

But this woman had her measurements. She wanted me to cut her ten-foot-long, four-inch-diameter PVC pipe into ten-*inch* sections. My first mental reaction was to say, *Fuck you*. My first verbal comment was, "Ah, no, I'm not going to do that."

She was not only shocked by my refusal but also grew irritated, and said, "Well, how am I going to get my project done, if you aren't going to do this?" I told her we sold saws, and pointed up the aisle.

She was really put off by my effrontery, as she saw it—imagine having to actually saw something yourself for your own project! She then looked at me with earnest arrogance and told me that she would then not be buying the PVC pipe at all, and added that she would buy it somewhere else. I think she said this to shock me into the reality of the lost sale, and that I would then cut it for her. She stood standing, defiantly, waiting for me to relent in my refusal. But in response to her telling me she was leaving I just said "OK," and she turned and stormed up the aisle and threw the PVC pipe in the pile.

This, Dear Reader, is not aberrant behavior. It is daily behavior.

As I mentioned, the word "project" is the last word most associates want to hear. Many people just want you, the associate, to do the thinking for them. This is apart from those customers who want you to take them through the entire plumbing of their house and how to install or repair things, as there are a good amount of people who don't want to pay a plumber. A fellow plumbing associate, Mark, who was a plumber, stops people in the middle of these attempted conversations, and tells them they need to get a plumber. The people stare in disbelief for a couple of seconds, before walking off, dejected.

Sometimes you get lucky, though. Sometimes when you hear the word "project," your fears of a forty-five-minute-or-more encounter with the customer become unwarranted, and it is over very quickly. The person knows what he or she wants, and just needs a little extra assistance in thinking through a couple of things. This is no problem.

However, sometimes you will get a combination of the "project" person and the person attempting to build something, or basically cobbling it together, and he or she is in way over his or her head, and he or she usually isn't aware of it. Cobbled-together installations or repairs are called "cob-jobs." Cob-jobs are usually done by inexperienced people, people who don't have a lot of money (though it will cost more in the long run), people who like duct tape, or by cheap repairmen who overcharge the customers and do shoddy work. As a friend of mine has said when telling me of a cob-job, it really doesn't take more than a couple extra minutes to think things through and do them right.

A few of the cob-jobbers will come into the store at infrequent intervals, especially as they're knee-deep in some project going wrong or about to go wrong. I will frequently hide, literally, when I see them coming. The spaces between and behind water heaters make for nice enclosures.

But I do get caught by the cob-jobbers. I'd like to now detail one such encounter.

A very hyperactive man in his midforties, smelling of marijuana, with red eyes to boot, came up to me in the plumbing aisle. He had a project. He stood about five feet, four inches tall and weighed around 135 pounds. He had short brown hair, which contained the drag marks from his comb. He had also read a book on plumbing, or was in the middle of a book on plumbing.

He explained to me that he was putting in a kind of tub and shower, but the space he was putting it in was too cramped for a full bath. He was making a kind of short and low bath, really meant more for a shower, but much too long and narrow. It sounded like only a child would be able to use it. (But, of course, the person he was building it for was not a child). It took me a while to figure out what he was saying, because when I encounter a customer I immediately think he or she is doing it the right way, and I make mental notes from this perspective. When I get confused, it usually means that I'm not listening fully, the customer isn't explaining things fully, or the customer is cob-jobbing. The cob-job customer takes you out of your normal thinking process, and has you imagine the possibilities of what he or she is trying to do.

And this is exactly what the dope-smoking, hyperactive, amateur plumber said to me: "I need you to imagine the possibilities." He stared intensely at me while he said this. I looked away.

He pulled a photograph of the "tub and shower" out of his pocket, and began to explain the problem he was having, centered around the overflow pipe for the tub. He couldn't use a typical tub drain assembly, as he needed the overflow plate and trip lever—the part you flip up and down to keep water in or out of the tub—to be further out into the tub due to some impediment behind it. We walked back and forth from one aisle to the next, as his imagination grew.

After a good half hour of his shenanigans, I told him what he had in mind should work, the lever would probably still operate.

He lost his photograph of his tub, and asked me three times if I had it. I said I didn't know where it was. He left and came back, and then told me he found it. He also told me he'd call if he needed more help.

I didn't see him again for over a month. Unfortunately, I was concentrating on shelving furnace filters when he appeared at my side. He told me, still agitated, still with the sweet stink of marijuana, that he was running into problems with the spout on the tub. It wasn't long enough.

I couldn't believe he was still working on installing the tub, over a month later. But there were problems. He told me that he had installed a rubber liner, used for shower base installations, and had cut it into the sizes he wanted, to seal off the sides of the shower-tub thing he was building. The shower-tub thing already had ceramic tile over the unsealed rubber liner abutting in the corners. He had a new picture.

He told me the water was running out the cracks and it had damaged the wooden sub-flooring so much that he had to replace it. There were additional things that went wrong because of the water, but I won't go into them. It's best just to imagine someone taking two steps backward for every step forward.

He had now rearrived at the store because the overflow-plate-with-trip lever was jutting out too far, so much so that he needed to extend the spout above it even further past it, so the water could land in the tub.

I had nothing to offer him, and I told him that. I said that they don't make things for what you're doing, because nobody does what you're doing. He said he understood, but that he needed me to think of the possibilities again. So, begrudgingly, I did that.

I told him he could just solder on an extra piece of copper to extend it, but he told me that the copper was too close to the stud, and that he didn't feel comfortable doing that.

So I told him all he could do was use a compression fitting, run galvanized pipe from the female pipe side of the compression fitting, and then go into his spout from there. He said it would work, but that he would then need the base of the spout to not be as wide as everything we had in stock, due to a strange protuberance he showed me in the new tub picture.

"What's that?" I asked.

He began to explain in great detail, very rapidly, but I just stopped him and told him we didn't have anything else other than regular tub spouts.

"Work with me here," he said. "And I want something nice, too. Something classy. Do you have anything in chrome?"

I had already told him twice that we didn't have anything, period, and so I explained this again. I thought to myself, "If we don't have anything at all, sir, that *includes no chrome*."

He began shuffling around near the inline shutoffs, the shutoff valves people have in their basements. They are all brass, usually with red handles.

He repeated to himself, "Anything at all in chrome? I want it to look nice."

As a joke, I mentioned that the only thing we have in chrome are the regular under-sink shutoffs.

"Lead the way," he said.

I took him to the chrome-plated shutoffs. These shutoffs are about three inches long, maybe one inch high. They come with a rather flimsy oval handle and a noticeable white plastic stem.

I really couldn't believe he was actually thinking about using this for his tub spout.

He picked one up, turned it around in his hand—I forgot to mention he was dramatic as well—and asked me what I thought.

I told him I thought he should put it down and go to a plumbing supply shop.

He didn't want to pay the extra money, he said.

Yet he wants something nice? I thought to myself.

I asked him whether he realized that the water for his "tub" would be coming out of a three-eighths-inch opening, and not the large opening tub spouts usually have. I also mentioned this would mean that it would take three times as long to fill up his "tub." He said he understood, adding, "I think this may just work."

When I told my friend—a contractor experienced in plumbing—about the man and the story above, I asked him what he would have said to him. My usually kind, passive, lighthearted friend said, "I would have grabbed him by his ear and taken him to the exit, kicked him in his ass, and told him to get the hell out of here." I told him I thought that was good. Though, at the time, I said, I had other things in mind.

Ear Man
Victor Gischler

When I graduated from the University of Central Florida with a bachelor's degree in Radio & Television and a minor in Creative Writing, I had roughly the same job prospects as, say, a lump of coal or perhaps a dead pigeon. Majoring in radio and television pretty much taught me I'd lost all interest in radio and television. And no matter how many times I scoured the classifieds, I never saw a listing for a would-be sci-fi author. Back then, that's what I wanted to be. My brain had grown nerdy and fat on *Star Trek* and *Space: 1999* reruns. I'd seen *Star Wars* six thousand times. Yeah, I was one of those guys. Not ashamed to say it. Still *am* one of those guys if you want to know the truth.

I digress.

I had bills, expenses, student loans, but no job. I was offered a job. I didn't want it, but I took it anyway. Selling hearing aids. *What?* Ha, that old joke. Tell somebody you sell hearing aids, and you'll hear that joke every day for the rest of your life. "I sell hearing aids." *What?* Sometimes they'd cup their hands to their ears and say it. *What?* I used to think the world was full of comedians. Now I know it's really filled with the same comedian over and over again, all passing around the same joke book. *What?* Go to hell.

I digress. It happens. Back to the job.

The person who offered me this job was my stepfather. My stepfather is one hell of a good guy and a crackerjack salesman. He brought me in, showed me how to give the hearing test. Raise a finger when you hear the beep. A chimp could do this job. Seriously. You mark red *x*'s or blue *o*'s on a chart. The *x*'s and *o*'s correspond to the volume level to which the patient hears the beep. Different frequencies. Raise a finger. Child's play. Chimp's play. Giving the hearing test was the easy part. Getting the patient to plunk down eighteen hundred bucks for a pair of hearing aids was another story. That took courage. I didn't like looking some old lady in the eye and saying, "Get out your checkbook. This is going to sting a little." But these old folks have money. Not all of them. Of course not. But more than you think. They squirrel it away. But, man, they don't want to part with it.

I learned the following at a hearing-aid-sales seminar: You have to come around on a customer five times to get the highest possible sales percentage. That means even if they say "no" four times, you have to pitch them a fifth time. If you work on commission, you don't eat if you don't sell. Five times. It goes like this:

"You should buy this hearing aid."

"No."

"Sir, you've got a high-frequency loss, and you're missing a number of words, important words in everyday conversations. It's time to get these hearing aids."

"No."

"Sir, you're making it hard on your loved ones. They want to communicate with you. They love you. Don't you want to hear the happy words of your shining grandchildren? Let's fit you for some hearing aids today."

"No."

"You want to hear better, don't you?"

"Yes."

"Then let's fit you with some state-of-the-art custom hearing aids."

"No."

"We both know you need these hearing aids, so stop farting around and get out your checkbook."

"OK."

In theory, that's how it's supposed to go. Beat on them, bludgeon them, come around five times, and they eventually cave. Sometimes it even worked.

The machine you use to give this hearing test is called an Audiometer. You've probably seen such a device hooked up to a glass, soundproof booth. Maybe in the mall. They have portable ones too. That's how I got started, driving all around Butt-fuck, Egypt, with a portable Audiometer in my truck. People would call an 800 number because they saw a commercial on cable television, and this phone call would produce a "lead." You've seen *Glengarry Glen Ross*, right? Same thing. We'd work over these leads and set up appointments and drive out and do the test and hopefully make a sale.

Here is a real, actual phone call as best I can remember it:

OLD LADY (*answers phone*): Hello?

ME: Hello, Mrs. X, I'm a hearing specialist from Hearing Aid Company, and you recently expressed some interest in improving your hearing. I wanted to call to see if I could answer any questions you might have.

OLD LADY: It's mostly in my left ear. People mumble. I can't hear the TV.

ME: Sounds like I might need to come out there and give you a hearing test.

(*At this point, we negotiate a day and a time, and I ask for directions.*)

OLD LADY: You know that street with the place?

ME: ?

OLD LADY: That place where you turn and it forks off.

ME: What's the name of the street?

OLD LADY: It's by the chain-link fence. The one with the barking dogs.

ME: The barking dogs?

OLD LADY: Turn at the barking dogs.

ME: What if they're not barking?

OLD LADY: They're always barking.

I have given hearing tests in noisy apartments with kids running around, in cabins out in the deep dark woods, in mobile homes and nursing homes. I put a lot of miles on the truck and on the Audiometer. I sold hearing aids.

Eventually I moved to the location in the mall. This meant I sat at the counter and typed on an electric typewriter and waited for customers to walk in. It wasn't supposed to work like that. I was supposed to stand out in the mall traffic and lure shoppers into the soundproof booth for a free hearing test. Instead, I sat at the typewriter and wrote the first story for which I was ever paid money.

The story was called "Conquering the Andersons." It was about a kid who grew up in a mad scientist family and had to save his town from his berserk brother while his parents were away at a mad scientists' convention. The brother had built a large robotic cockroach from things in the garage and was terrorizing the town. I sold this story to a magazine called *Alternate Hilarities* for the princely sum of $25. I would have had to write and sell eight such stories to equal the commission on one hearing aid. But I was a writer. A paid writer.

I digress. I would not get the news that the story had been accepted for some time. At the moment, I was still sitting at the typewriter instead of pushing hearing aids on mall shoppers. What I did not realize was that my stepfather was around the corner watching me. Watching me not sell hearing aids. The simple fact of the matter was that I didn't want to sell hearing aids, could not picture myself growing old and retiring and regaling my grandchildren with my amazing hearing-aid-selling adventures.

But my stepdad was, and is, a good man, and I still feel bad, thinking about the disappointment he must have felt, watching me type my little story. My stepdad took care of my mom and my sister and me, all of us, by selling hearing aids.

I went back to grad school soon after that. My stepfather probably breathed a sigh of relief. Looking back over the years, that little chunk in my life, the time I sold hearing aids, seems now sort of like a digression. A bump in the road on my way to being a professional writer. But I learned something about myself and about people in general, something hard to put into words, but I know I'd be a different person now if I hadn't sold hearing aids, learned how to operate an Audiometer, and shirked my job to write a fairly silly story for twenty-five bucks. We are all the accumulation of our experiences. I believe it was Shakespeare who said . . .

Ah, but I digress. Always, always I digress.

Deviant You, Deviant Me
C.A. Conrad

The bookstore I work at has been my laboratory for analyzing, diagnosing, and treating assholes of all shapes and sizes. I'm an asshole specialist. I ask you, where the fuck is my PhD? All the work I've done in my field must not go unrewarded! If you're an asshole and I get a whiff of you, you'll know I know, trust me. There will be no doubt in your mind that I know, but you will have no evidence to take to a manager to have me fired. I'm not passive-aggressive, I'm aggressive-passive, something like a hooded executioner. I'm that good! And you're that dead!

I hate working, and want to change this world as best I can while I'm alive, but I'm just not sure how to make those changes. It's all wrong, jobs are a stupid idea for a planet, for living, for being human. Love and the creative must come together. For instance, I know from my years of studying assholes that assholes didn't start out as assholes. In fact it's my expert opinion that assholes don't even like being assholes, but are so configured by their daily asshole behavior that no other way of life seems possible to them anymore. Love is forgotten all over the world, and assholes appear. Creativity is lacking. The core is not entirely rotten, just hollow. But sometimes the stench of rot overwhelms, like these nasty customers who blame everyone and everything for their misery, including the weather. What to do with these assholes?

How can snow be your enemy when you wear mink and live in a $2,000,000 condominium? All those beautiful little animals died to make your coat but you still bitch about the cold! Have you never seen a photograph of a snowflake? Have you never considered these snow crystals have come through miles of sky to land on your tongue? By the way, are you aware that Philadelphia is far enough north of the equator that we are supposed to have snow? Have you considered Florida? Please consider Florida, because let me tell you, if I were a mink with the knowledge of taxidermy, *oooh!* I hate this store, I hate it.

Some days I can't believe my job is part of my life. It's so painful, and I stand there ignoring everyone and *pray* for the Angel of Death to snatch me off my feet! It's the crazy people I like the most at the store, the homeless, obsessive, lonely ones who wander through the door after a day of panhandling. Like the giant man in the one-piece green suit who carries a small handful of books from the second floor to the third floor over and over, unnoticed during our busiest hours. Then finally we find that he's been stacking several hundred books in piles up there. He says he has no idea why he's doing it, but we can't be angry with him, even though it takes over an hour to put the books back into their different sections: self-help, Christianity, diet, real estate. He's a gentle giant. I like the crazy people because I like myself. I love them like family I don't visit much, but talk to on the phone once in a while on those occasions when I feel ugly and awkward around the general population. It's when I need contact with someone who reminds me I'm OK—crazy—but OK.

There's a homeless woman who figured out how to use our PA system, and one day we heard her for a glorious one and a half minutes all over the store at *top volume*, "AAAY! YOU THINK YOU'RE SPECIAL!?" Every single person in the store looked to the ceiling as this *huge* voice shot from the speakers, "YOU'RE NOT SO SPECIAL! AAAY! MOTHERFUCKER! FUCKER! FUCKER! AAAY! YOU THINK YOU KNOW IT ALL!? FUCKER! YOU KNOW NOTHING! FUCKER! YEAH! AAAY! FUCKER! HEY GIVE ME THAT! LEAVE ME ALONE! THAT'S MINE" The music comes back on, everyone laughs. They laugh, but I know she knows what she's saying, yes, oh yes. The security guards have her by either arm on the escalator and she is smiling. Then I hear her laughing. She's laughing and I can hear her laughter even after she's out of sight. I like her most of all. Her name is Angela, and she's a Pisces. And I want to start a bloodless revolution with her. We can change the world, Angela. But I can't help thinking *how* they would stop us. I need you, you need me.

Tulip Thief
Gary Mex Glazner

I worked as a florist for eighteen years, but always wanted to do something more masculine, so I became a poet. However, there were manly aspects and moments on the job.

"Call 911," I yelled over my shoulder as I ran towards the door. Someone had been stealing plants and flowers from the display in front of the store. In order to help sales and make the store more attractive, we had been putting plants and flowers on the sidewalk in front of the store, giving it the feel of a French country village. We had bales of hay and buckets of pink lilies that had a fragrance that was a cross between first girl-friend and just-cooked pie. We had bright red azaleas in an old wooden wheelbarrow, and an A-frame sign with balloons and the daily special written in chalk. It was inviting and had been working to increase sales, but things had been disappearing: a green plant here, a blooming plant there, next a bunch of flowers. From my workstation, where I arranged flowers, I could look through the glass doors and front display window. I had made a mental note to keep my eyes open to see when the thief would next strike. A man was walking by, didn't even slow down, bent a little, and scooped up a fire-orange tulip plant and kept walking.

By the time I got out the door he was at the end of the

block. He wasn't looking back and I was picking up speed. I had played football in junior high school and knew how to tackle. I lowered my shoulder and hit him waist high. He had stopped at the light and was waiting to cross the street. I was sprinting and hit him solid with all my weight. He moaned soft and low like a cow being hit with a baseball bat. The tulip plant popped loose from his grasp and broke on the ground, dirt spilling, and red clay pot-shards splintering. He lost his balance and went down, smacking the cement sidewalk. I grabbed him by his shirt collar and said, "You are under citizen's arrest." I got him to his feet and started walking him to the police station, which was down one block and around the corner. He came willingly for about half a block until we got back in front of the flower shop. Then he came out of his daze and saw I wasn't joking and had really placed him under arrest and was walking him to the police station.

There was always pressure to make the shop profitable; every night we talked about how to increase sales, about how to make sure we made a profit, about doing profit and loss reports, and now here I was on the ground about to kill or at least seriously hurt one of our customers. He was a regular customer and had been stealing plants and flowers for about two weeks, he confessed. Margaret walked up to him and yelled, "You are a regular customer for God's sake, why are you stealing from us?" He just looked up kind of embarrassed and shy, nodding his head that he didn't know why he had stolen the plant. He was drunk and it had worked before and seemed so harmless.

He began to struggle and try to slip out of my grasp. I wrestled him to the ground and a crowd began to form. I yelled again, "Call 911." Margaret and the other flower shop employees yelled back as a chorus, "We did, we did, the cops are on the way." I was on top of him and he started to struggle more and raised his fist to hit me. "Stay down motherfucker," I screamed in his face. A woman came up to me and screamed, "You are using excessive use of force." "Get away from me you fucking bitch," I replied. He started to get loose. I raised my fist and screamed, "Stop moving or I'll smash your face." He stopped moving. Bob the barber came over and I again yelled, "Call the police." Bob said, "We did, they are on the way," and he kneeled down and placed his knee on the guy's chest. The crowd began to chant, "Hit him, hit him!" This made him struggle more, and again I raised my fist, this time thrusting it down like I was going to punch him, pulling away only at the last moment. I thrust it down at him again and again made him flinch.

Florists are part psychologists. People rarely buy flowers unless they are in a heightened emotional state. They are falling in love, or they have had a big fight, or a baby, or they want to seduce someone, or someone has died. People look to florists to help them choose the right bouquet to express their feelings, to accomplish those goals. What color says "sex me up"? What is the fragrance that says "bye Mom"? People want you to help write their love notes, although after you make a suggestion, they will often say, "No, she's not that kind of woman," and grab the pen and say, "Alright, let me do it." They just want permission to be gushy. Once while I was taking an order, a woman asked me what she should say after the best night of lovemaking of her career, and if I thought guys liked roses. She decided her card should say, "Thank you for eight hours of orgasms."

Right now I wanted to give Mr. Tulip Thief a cactus garden. I was sitting on top of him, and time slowed down and each moment was long and clear. I was delivery boy, manager, arranger, owner, and super-flower-man, all in one.

On my first day working at the shop, on the last delivery run of the day, I knocked a bunch of times and finally a young woman came to the door. She had wet hair and a wet T-shirt and unbuttoned cut-off jeans, her pubic hair peeking out of the top of the cut-offs. She apologized for taking so long, saying, "Sorry it took so long, I was in the hot tub." It never happened again in eighteen years of deliveries, and only once did I use citizen's arrest.

Sweeping the sidewalk in front of the shop was my favorite part of the job. I would go out in the morning before the store opened. It was calming and peaceful and gave me a sense of ownership of the street. I was the sheriff of Grant Avenue. I protected that street. It was my street. I took care of it with my sweeping and by saying good morning to people. I was a happy, smiling, small-town business owner, upstanding member of Rotary, a total professional, completely committed to customer service. The customer is always right, even if sometimes they have to be dragged down the street screaming.

When would the police get here? Where were they? How could it take so long for the police to arrive? The station was just around the block. I had grown up next door to Sergeant Rick Rudy and the chief of police was a regular customer, sending flowers to his sweetheart, who was a big, blond, busty L.A. police officer. The cops were my friends, my really slow friends.

The streets, which were normally empty, now had crowds of

people all waiting to see if there would be violence. People spilled out of the movie theater, the deli, the car repair place, the jewelry store, the two barbershops, and even Rick's World Wide Web Café. Meanwhile people were saying, "Do you think he will hit him?" "I bet he will hit him." "He's gonna hit him." The street was buzzing and they offered encouragement. "Hit him! Hit him!"

The flower shop was a family business and I started as delivery boy, then became a clerk, answering the phone and taking orders, then learned to make flower arrangements as a designer. After ten years, my parents wanted to retire and I bought the shop from them on credit and paid off the loan over five years. The last three years I knew I wanted to sell the store and use the money to travel around the world to learn about poetry and to use the cushion to make the change from florist to full-time poet.

Time at the shop felt like being in prison. Even though I could come and go and the money was good, especially in owning the business, to go to the same fifteen hundred square feet and do the same tasks over and over for decades was living-dead, zombie work. I wanted out—bad. Every time I said I was a florist, I cringed. Selling flowers is cyclical, especially with flowers for the holidays, year after year, hundreds of pine bough Christmas centerpieces, fall flowers in cornucopias with orange oak leaves and red roses—yes, we have red roses.

I told the tulip thief that, "Historically, flowers were used at funerals to cover the smell of the dead." He looked at me like I was crazy. I felt we were bonding; perhaps I was losing myself in him, falling in love? Lying in the street on the black tar, white line, center of town, a few feet from the front door of the flower shop. The shop was in a block of retail stores built in the 1930s and next door to a movie theater with a huge red and white marquee. The shop had four big display windows and a white metal awning. The awning had support bars that were just right for a kid to jump up and swing on. The landlord had wrapped the support bars in barbwire and people were always jumping up and grabbing on, only to find their hand being gouged and cut by the barbwire. For years a piece of dried flesh hung from one of the support bars.

All the rage of being an owner's child was pouring into my fists. Smash his face, was what I thought. Was I thinking at all? Sitting on a man's chest in the middle of the road, I was red-faced and exploding, convincing him to stay down. I was berserk and filled with eighteen years of sweeping the same sidewalk over and over, the same leaves, seedpods, cigarettes, and small-town dust. I would just as soon kill him as say, "Novato Florist, may I help you?" Say it one more time, say it ten thousand more times, still say it under my breath when I answer any phone. "May I help you!?"

He was humiliated by my masculinity, my flower-ness, my stamen, and my stem. Laugh at me every time I say I am florist. No one was laughing now! People always say, "You work in a forest?" "Not forest, florist." My college professor Ellen said it: "You mean with trees and nuts and birds?" Now all of that was purring inside me and I was Lizard Brain and Protect-Territory Skull, holding a tulip thief on the sweet black street. He was dirty blond and skinny and scared shitless that a man had tackled him, dragged him down the street, and was threatening to beat him to a pulp. He had a dirty white shirt on that was showing serious sweat stains.

The cops came, four cars with two men in each car, Sergeant Rudy leading the charge, guns drawn, ready to shoot. They wanted to know what happened and were very interested when I said "I put him under citizen's arrest" and they say, "Did you put him under citizen's arrest?" "Yes, take him away," I said, and they said yes and put him in the patrol car and drove the half block and turned and parked in front of the station and took him inside.

Later, a policeman came back to the store to fill out a report. He said, "What happened?" I said, "A man walked by, grabbed a tulip plant, I tackled him and put him under citizen's arrest, and then you took him away." He said, "How much do you think the tulip plant was worth?" I said, "About $3.50 wholesale, we sell it for $15."

He said, "Tulip. How do you spell that?"

Klaus
Timothy Bracy

I worked for five years at the Chesapeake Muffin and Coffee Shop in suburban Washington, D.C. I loved working at the coffee shop, because, amongst other things, there was quite a cast of characters. There was Mitya, the imperious Russian. There was Stramboul, the Algerian who would touch your back, shoulders, and sides as he passed behind you. There was the always sexy Rawerna. And many others. The experience was rich and transporting—I felt I was living in a novel. But then Klaus came and ruined it for me.

Klaus arrived shortly after the business was sold to Mr. Uger. Whether Mr. Uger regrets his hiring to this day I cannot say with any certainty, for I have not seen Mr. Uger in some time. But I still believe he has a good heart, and despite the occurrence of events that permanently scarred me, I continue to wish him the best.

Not so charitable, my feelings for Klaus. He arrived in the late summer, like a fever that wouldn't break. He said he was an exchange student from Austria, but I never saw any evidence to that effect. No books, no discernible routine either day or night. Klaus seemed a bit old to be a student anyway—late fifties perhaps—although he kept the bowl haircut of a little boy. He was tall and reedy, with enormous hands and a ruddy, spectacled face. He dressed immaculately in his way—cardigan sweaters and tweed jackets, billowing slacks and loafers—all of which caused him to look not professorial, but like a pastiche, an intellectual caricature. I am unable to explain why precisely this made me so angry, for I was not above a little academic pretense myself—holding forth on various philosophical esoterica, a little Hegel here and a bit of classical Greek—while preparing lattes and skim decaf cappuccinos. But with Klaus, there was artifice, malignance. Klaus wasn't interested in the classics—that much was obvious immediately. His true tastes ran a little more towards, shall we say, the "latest hits."

You should know that I am not a man given to great sentimentality. During my years I have cast my tender devotions rather sparingly—a romance here and there, some affection for a parent or uncle, and of course my one true love: the Chesapeake Muffin and Coffee Shop. Understand that while my compensation was quite adequate, it was not for money that I served my customers. To the contrary: If I found that a week would pass, or a month even, when I did not receive any kind of remuneration for my long hours—which was only too often the case—I would always endure this wordlessly, and with an eye towards the greater well-being of the enterprise. This burden of suffering I took upon myself quite joyously, and I was indeed uplifted when my "payday" would come, and I would find my employee box empty, save for maybe an amendment to the upcoming schedule which would cause me to have to rise at 4:00 AM the following morning to open up the shop. Such was the profound and ritual nature of my dedication.

I am also a welcoming soul. Whenever a new employee was hired, it was my self-motivated disposition to "take them under my wing" so that owing to my kind and experienced auspices, they could come to know the ins and outs of what I liked to think of as "the coffee life." It was no small gesture, given that the shop had as many complex moving parts as a Mahler symphony and no unaffiliated human could be expected to master its challenges without the greatest degree of edifying guidance. In this way, at the risk of sounding a touch elevated in my self-regard—I was something of an oracle. None should desire to pass through these walls bereft of my tutelage. That I would provide this training was unspoken. I received no extra payment or acknowledgment, nor did I ask for any. But when I was customarily courteous enough to extend my lessons to the newcomer Klaus, he rather . . .

But OK—let me say it now (I think the coast is clear): Mr. Uger is responsible for the drastic decline of this once decent coffee shop, which had served the community well for many years. There—I said it. That is where the blame lies: Uger and Klaus. And even if they are nearby, I am no longer afraid of them, despite whatever unconscionable deeds were committed in the basement.

One time I was not paid for two or three months! I no longer remember whether I was recompensed for the checks that bounced or the banking fees they engendered. I have been through and seen a lot: two weeks straight with no breaks and three doubles, working alone at a job which once required two, three, four. For close to a year I received no raise in pay while tripling my productivity and responsibility. Why was it the case that I was pushed to these physical and mental extremes—so much so that I felt at times I was going truly insane? Was all my labor just to fund and finance the howling and singing? Yes: the singing. When I was working long shifts at the counter, I began to hear Klaus sing from the basement a sweet and merry jingle, like something that might emanate from an ice-cream truck as it serviced all the children down a crowded suburban street. I could not make out all of the words—some of them seemed to be in German—but the cheerful chorus always stayed with me: "Downstairs, downstairs, don't ever ever go downstairs . . . "

Also understand this, I beseech you. You must know that when Uger took over, things were very shortly not the same. Soon the premises were anarchic. A bedlam took hold that frightened me. Mr. Uger was a cagey man of Eastern European extraction, a recent immigrant who quickly took to running the shop in the fashion of his lesser-resourced homeland. Corners were cut. Items were often in short supply. And not just trivial, ancillary things either. For instance, from time to time we would run out of coffee. A shipyard should never be without seaworthy craft, and a coffee shop never without coffee. Such shortfalls would lead to vexing, hurtful exchanges such as these:

> CUSTOMER: Well since you don't have small or medium cups, I suppose I will make it a large coffee.
>
> ME: I'm sorry, but we've run out.
>
> CUSTOMER: Excuse me? You are out of coffee? But you're a coffee shop!

ME: Could I make you an espresso drink?

The enormity of my shame was nearly impossible to quantify. It made me want to take some action—drastic, impertinent. Tables were covered in muffin crumbs. Used and unused napkins were pathetically splayed beneath the tables. God forbid I was asked for my recommendation! The bread is stale, the muffins are stale . . . I cannot recommend anything and when customers ask I always tell them—juice.

Along these lines, my anxiety grew day by day. There was always a line of customers six deep and now and then a party of four arrived, pushing the line out of the door into the wet elements. They were always smiling, cheerful and unaware of the kind of treatment they were about to receive. From me, from Klaus, from Uger.

I was alone behind the counter, telling a customer we had neither decaffeinated coffee or herbal teas, hadn't for weeks, for which I could find no plausible excuse. I was weary, sweating, stumbling, exhausted. Behind me, two bagels had popped from the toaster, both needing cream cheese, and a smoothie was in a blender, waiting to be served. Out of the corner of my eye, I saw its intended recipient: he was looking to the blender then to me, wondering why I didn't just put it in the cup. I then saw the people at the table who had already waited ten minutes for their bagel. I also saw the people by the couches, still waiting on their sandwiches. Then to my left, a sudden explosion: I had forgotten that the steam wand was broken and a torrent of boiled and unusable soy milk had spread all over the counters and floors. Nearby, the door to the refrigerator was open, oozing air, a clutter of plastic plates and food items—cucumbers, tomatoes, turkey, roast beef. In better days I would have looked at this as a despicable energy waste. Now it hardly merited attention. Klaus had left for a fifteen-minute break forty minutes ago. Where was he?

The customer waiting for the bagels pointed to his wrist: It's time. I assured the customer at the register that an Americano is very similar to a regular coffee and that I would not charge him extra for it and have it ready in no time. I moved the bagels and quickly slathered one with cream cheese, but found there was not enough to cover the second. I called down the stairs for Klaus: "Klaus, could you bring me up some cream cheese?" but there was no formal reply. Only the singing. And then a howl. I put more soy milk into the decanter and set that into the steamer. I checked the sandwiches, none of which, to my relief, were burnt and began setting out plates with chips when I heard behind me an exasperated sigh—the smoothie. I quickly poured the smoothie into the cup. The customer received it with a blank, angry stare, and then left wordlessly. "Klaus?" I said still louder, "Could you bring me up some cream cheese?"

No answer.

"Are the muffins fresh today?" "No." "Do you have the chicken sandwich?" "No." "Do you have any of that cheesecake?" "No." "Do you have the salad at least?" "We do in a sense but I wouldn't today—no." "Well, do you have anything?" "Well—do you like juice?"

Now, I want to tell you something funny. Shops are amusing this way—sometimes you hear a strange thing from a fellow employee that maybe you weren't intended to hear. One Tuesday while I was closing, I eavesdropped on a conversation between Mitya and Rawerna: "Did you realize that Klaus has given himself a raise?"

Well! Understand how this surprised me! As a jumble and word game enthusiast, I couldn't help but be struck by this irresistible puzzle. While I had been working tirelessly and without respite for weeks at a time—a labor which yielded no salary—I had scarcely seen Klaus at all. And I had further believed all this time that only Uger was of significant rank and standing to call for a raise. And yet Klaus simply provided one to himself? I was completely bamboozled!

As I stood at the milk steamer the phone rang. It used to ring often with orders for take-out sandwiches; now it was only creditors and distressed former employees.

"Is Uger there?"

"No."

"Don't you fucking cover for him."

"I've got like one thousand orders here and a line out the door, sir, could you just call back?"

"No. Put him on the fucking phone."

This kind of rough talk was occurring with greater and greater frequency at the shop. Frustrated customers, irritable staff—they swore constantly. I did not like this sense of diminishing aesthetics, the loss of refinement. It no longer felt to me like we were providing any sort of service to the community. To the contrary: Our particular block of this quiet neighborhood was gradually turning seedier. A pawnshop moved in across the street, advertising firearms and discount appliances. The following month, three doors down in the same shopping center, an "Adult Superstore" opened, promising to meet any and all requirements for "progressive lovemaking," whatever that meant.

Staff turnover was becoming an issue. Stramboul's visa ran out and he was forced to return to Algeria. Mitya bristled against the new regime, complained repeatedly, and eventually took a job across town at the Gooseberry Tea Supply. I missed my friends and imagined that new employees would be hired to take their place . . . but none ever were. Instead I found myself working longer and longer shifts, a development that was entirely unremarked upon by Uger. In fact he rarely seemed to be in the shop at all these days. His basement office, the one he had previously occupied, now was the province of Klaus, who insisted whenever he surfaced that he was doing "paperwork." It all felt strange to me: Uger gone, Klaus in the office night and day, the howling, the singing. I wanted to grab Klaus one time by the lapels, to shake and scream at him, "Where is Uger?! Where is he, sloth?" But for whatever reason, I was unable to summon the fortitude to do so.

Finally, after several weeks, one incident steeled in me my resolve to see what was happening downstairs.

It was around eleven thirty in the morning, that time when every Saturday there was a five-minute lull with absolutely no customers, just before the lunch rush began in earnest. I should have been taking this opportunity to clean up and restock, but I was feeling physically sick and mentally unstable—instead I went outside to smoke. Not thirty seconds into what would be the only break in my twelve-hour day, a passerby observed me with my tobacco and told me it was disgusting. I nodded in assent, the assessment seeming unfair but true. But who then should appear but Ted.

Ted did not respect me. He was a former employee who had recently resigned, and he knew no self-respecting person would ever put himself through this. He had left. He'd quit. He'd actually done something. He didn't just stand there and take it. Weakness, irresolution, softness: The best employees left within a month of Uger's coming. Why was I still here? Ted had come back though, for his tips.

TED: Is Uger here?

ME: I haven't seen him in weeks . . . why?

TED: I want my tips. Are they ready?

ME: I don't know, I'm busy.

TED: Did you get your tips?

ME: Could you come back? The tips are not my affair. That's Klaus's department.

TED: Now I get it, now I see.

The truth was there were no tips anymore. All of them, for some reason, now went to Klaus. The inequity wreaked ruin on my sense of fair play—what had once been a highly egalitarian concern was now most egregiously slanted towards a privileged few. And I was just a cog. Klaus was a puppet master, Uger vanished, presumably not returning, and I was left to hold the shop together entirely on my own. As of the final week of the summer, besides Klaus, I was the sole full-time employee of the Chesapeake Muffin and Coffee. And yet I could not understand it and resolved to walk down and address the matter myself with Uger, if he were in fact on the premises, or, if need be, Klaus. But that very night the singing was louder than ever:

"Downstairs, downstairs, don't ever ever go downstairs . . . "

I Scream
Colson Whitehead

Mine is the story of a man who hates ice cream and of the world that made him.

I was once like you, always quick with a "two scoops, please" and a "whipped cream, damn it, whipped cream!" I loved a Breyers vanilla-chocolate-strawberry rectangle straight from the freezer. Never mind if it was a bit long in the tooth, nestled in there next to a half-empty bag of carrots-and-peas medley—scrape off the icy fur and it was good to go. Orange sherbet? Cool. In Baskin-Robbins, I used pure willpower to persuade the red digital lights of the Now Serving machine to announce my number, which was a sweat-smudged blob on the pink paper strip in my quivering hand. You can keep your Kiwi Mocha Bombasta; the nuclear-green sludge of mint chocolate chip was as exotic as it got, and that's how I liked things.

Then I went to work in an ice cream store.

I started scooping at Big Olaf in 1985. Sag Harbor, on the east end of Long Island, was still early in its Hamptonization. *Page Six* couldn't find it on a map, Schiavoni's Market didn't stock sushi, and Billy Joel wasn't driving into trees. Perhaps Big Olaf was a harbinger. When it opened on Sag Harbor's Long Wharf, it made quick work of its nearby competitor, the Tuck Shop, which had been the town's longstanding ice cream joint.

Big Olaf's secret weapon: the Belgian waffle cone, made before your very eyes. The smell of the batter haunts me still.

Most people think: Scooping ice cream, I could do that. But they don't understand the complexities, the high-stakes brinkmanship of the modern-day ice cream industry. You had to memorize the names and ever-shifting locations of the trendy flavors, this week's double-chunk whatever. You had to learn the ropes of the toppings bar and become a bit of a cop in the process, to keep the Heath bars from rumbling with the gummy bears. You had to figure out a solid scooping technique, no matter what the cost. As a teenage boy, I was seized by a potent suspicion that my right arm was growing bigger than my left. You can imagine what chiseling ice cream all day was doing for my self-consciousness.

Don't get me started on the Tofutti. I'm never going back to that place.

Most of all, you had to master all things waffle. There was a bit of theater involved in the making of the cones. You sat by the door on a special perch so that everyone could see you while you ladled batter onto the four waffle grills, which were mounted together on a wheel. Spin the wheel, remove the cone, roll it up, add more batter, spin the wheel, and on to the next. Move too fast and the cones peeled off limp and useless; move too slow and they turned out brittle and crumbled to dust when you looked at them.

And all the while, the hungry masses in bright polo shirts and pleated khaki shorts watched your every move, a mob eager for this spectacle of cone processing. The apparatus was probably leftover torture gear from some Belgian Cold War spy agency, unbolted from the floor of a basement interrogation room and shipped to the Hamptons. Where it found a home.

The perk of the job was all the ice cream you could eat, and ice cream was all I ate. There was a hot dog machine on site, where the franks spun eternally like grisly, grim planets, and occasionally I'd make a wretched feast of one, but most of the time I ate ice cream. Chocolate in a plastic cup with rainbow sprinkles, chocolate shakes, chocolate ice cream sodas, chocolate twist dispensed by a lever into wavy, brown, short-lived peaks.

For breakfast and lunch, or lunch and dinner, depending on my shift. For three long summers.

I was nauseated at the end of each day, but I persisted, never suspecting that I was conditioning myself to hate that which I so ardently desired. My metabolism is such that I did not suffer any physical effects from my gluttony. I was cursed in other ways: my aversion to ice cream, which spread quickly to most sweets, and then to all desserts.

When a person is offered dessert, a polite "I prefer not to" rarely does the trick. After hearing the details of how long my host labored over the apple brown Betty, it's hard to refuse a bite. (Not so hard that I actually have some, but hard nonetheless.) There is a cost, I'm saying.

Birthday parties and weddings force me to share my tales of Olafian woe with my incredulous companions, who shake their heads before asking if they can have my plate. Take it, take it all. Most people mistake the terrified expression on my face in my wedding photos as a sign of regret. In fact, my face records the horror at the knowledge that I must eat cake at some point or, in the post-cake-cutting photos, the utter revulsion over the spongy clump of frosted hell scraping through my gut.

It is no small thing to remove yourself from the world of

decent people. Predators abound. The natural enemies of the ice cream haters are the dessert fascists. You recognize them by the way they jab their little spoons at you from across the table, by the evangelical flourish with which they offer up their favorite phrases: "Have some," "You have to try this," "Trust me, you'll like it!"

Any resistance to their entreaties and they'll quickly turn on you. "How can you not like dessert?" they demand, and no excuse will calm these bullies. Your whole family could have been gunned down in some Ben & Jerry's massacre and they'll just wrinkle their noses and ask, "Not even one bite?"

To hate ice cream is to know dread at the clearing of the table, for at any moment the waiter will return with the dessert menu and put your nice evening to the test. Eventually you learn to compromise. Sometimes it is best to say, "I'll have a bite if you order something," and hope that your companions forget your promise. Most of the time they do—at the core of all dessert fascists is a frozen block of narcissism that will not melt. They don't want to share; they want affirmation of their choices.

Say what you will about ice cream haters—pity us, condemn us, take us off your guest list—but we don't need anyone's validation. We are content in ourselves, and at the feast of life, we happily dine alone.

How Swede It Was
Dealing Death by Pancakes in the Midwest
Randall Osborne

To cope with needy oldsters isn't so hard if you know you're killing them off at the same time, like we did in my parents' euthanasia shop.

It was in the early 1970s—Jack Kevorkian hadn't even started—when my mother and stepfather bought the Stockholm Inn, at Broadway and Twentieth Street, in Rockford, Illinois, open for breakfast, lunch, and dinner.

Our specialty: Swedish pancakes.

Not those lacy, crepe-like imposters you might have tried at IHOP, but real Swedish pancakes: loaded with eggs, browned on a greasy grill, folded steaming onto the football-shaped plate, and topped with twin gobs of butter.

Diners often asked for a side order of fat-squirting sausage links with their "super stack." Maybe another egg, too, over easy. Why not?

My stepfather Jim found the Stockholm Inn after he retired from his corporate job and went looking for something new. He brought us there for breakfast one weekend, so that we could scope the potential investment opportunity and test the goods. I chewed halfway through a short stack of Swedish pancakes. They were delicious but impossibly, artery-cloggingly rich.

I felt sick.

All around us, geriatrics forked into their super stacks. Some shouted for more butter. Low prices drew the social security crowd from all parts of town. The Stockholm Inn's no-liquor policy must have appealed to them as well.

I washed dishes. I bused tables. I stocked the basement shelves. It was my first job after high school.

Rockford's population, I figured, had only about six possible surnames—Johnson, Peterson, Carlson, Swenson, Lindberg, and Skarpsvärd. Their median age was eighty-five, and they drove barge-like Buicks very slowly through red lights, into the walls of buildings, and into each other. The city had more podiatrists than pay phones.

"Coffee," they barked. "Bring my coffee. And cream!" The waitresses were busy. I poured coffee. "Is this decaf? What?" Their hearing aids rolled onto the floor and crunched underfoot.

We had owned the Stockholm Inn for about a week when the first patron dropped dead—not in the restaurant, thankfully. Stuffed to his grey gills with you-know-what, the guy went down backwards like a finger-flicked wooden soldier in the Saturday sunlight, just outside the front door. My mother, frantic, called an ambulance. Paramedics pumped and shouted and bustled around the inert codger, then pulled the sheet over his head. Too late.

"I told you," I told my parents, again. I'd been insisting since we took over the Stockholm Inn that while we were doing a favor for the geezers and biddies of Rockford by providing them with cheap, tasty food at bargain prices, we were also pushing them faster toward their graves. "In a year or two, we'll have no customers left," I said.

Jim muttered, "Damn kid knows it all," and went downstairs to fix the walk-in cooler. Machinery was always breaking, which kept him busy, like he wanted. I did think I knew it all—except at those moments when I thought I didn't know anything and never would.

Most of the Stockholm Inn's clientele had partaken of Swedish pancakes for years without obvious ill effects. This, in my view, only made the likelihood stronger that we would soon start saying good-bye to them in droves. For good.

Some proved remarkably sturdy. Hard-hat crewmember Roger Gustafson would finish his daily stack at the back counter, spin on his stool, stand, and belch cavernously to the busy dining room. After a moment of almost reverent silence, the clink of silverware resumed. "Roger, please stop doing that," my mother told him. Roger squinted at her and nodded solemnly, his breath whistling out his nose. He stayed faithful to us—a belcher to the end—until his truck exploded into smithereens when he failed to beat the train at a crossing east of town. We couldn't bank on the likes of Roger, I thought.

Along with Swedish pancakes, we served seemingly more innocent dishes at lunch and dinner, such as *kroppkakor* (potato dumplings), Swedish pot roast, and the vile but much-adored lutfisk, which consists of whitefish that's been treated with lye, turning it into a jelly-like mass that smells like stale urine.

Our desserts were famous: bread puddings and cobblers, mostly, and in summer Madeline's fresh strawberry pie. One day I watched her slice berries into a bubbling sauce, and then splash a cascade of bright liquid into the mix. I read the label on the can.

"Red Dye No. 2!" I said, louder than I expected. The congressional hearings had made front pages everywhere. Red Dye

No. 2 , widely used in the food industry, was a proven carcinogen. The chemical name: trisodium 2 hydroxyl 1 sulphonato 4 napthylazo 1 napthelene 3 disulfonate 6. Regulators would ban it in 1976.

"Red Dye No. 2!" I said, pointing like an idiot.

"That's right, kid," Madeline grinned, and kept pouring.

Swedish pancakes promised a more dramatic death than Red Dye No. 2. The next casualty happened about a month after the first. Our man's dietary choices caught up with him as he climbed a small hill by the Stockholm Inn's back door. My mother wrung her hands. Paramedics performed their customary rigmarole. Too late.

"Don't say it," my mother told me, and stalked inside.

I pulled out another rack and poached my face in clouds of dishwasher steam. I hauled another bus pan to the kitchen. "Spoon!" some senior Sven shouted at my back, "I need a spoon!" I had visions of them giving out four, five, and six at once, when seated around a table or standing in line by the register.

"OK, I've decided to start looking at the whole situation differently," I told my mother. We had closed for the night. She counted money while Jim finished a wedge of strawberry pie. "Christ," Jim said. "Here goes the wise guy."

I said, "We think we're running a family restaurant, but we're really doing euthanasia. I mean, maybe their ride into the afterlife is not completely comfortable in every instance, so we can't strictly call it mercy killing. But we're saving people from drawn-out, wasting, painful deaths in hospitals." Jim scraped up the last of his Red Dye No. 2 pie. "Mostly."

My mother said I was very clever. She often told me this. Before long, I began to take it seriously and I would go on to suffer the consequences, but our Stockholm Inn era—that sepia-toned stage when I got into the swing of nutritional murder—stands as a period of exhausting fun. During our ownership, I'm pleased to report, nobody died in the dining room. Off-site keel-overs took place regularly, within about a half-block perimeter, but nothing that could easily be traced to our kitchen.

I came to know many of the grumpy old bastards by name. Most turned out to be gentle, bewildered, deaf Nordics. They just wanted, like the rest of us, to scoop something pleasant into the top ends of their bodies and crap it out the back, until the day they didn't have to anymore. One by one, they failed to show up for pancakes. We saw their obits in the newspaper.

But for every exterminated prospect, at least two more walk-ins discovered the Stockholm Inn. Business boomed. We rented the property next door and put in more seating.

A younger crowd appeared for lunch, guys in suits from the offices on Broadway. In a Robin Hood move, my mother marked up everything on the midday menu so that she could cut dinner prices even more. The mainstay was still breakfast—Swedish pancakes.

Three or four years felt like so many decades. My mother and Jim aged accordingly. When they couldn't take it anymore, they sold the Stockholm Inn. Red Dye No. 2 had been yanked from the market by then, but I think Madeline stockpiled plenty. Swedish pancakes were going strong. They are going strong today, though the Stockholm Inn has moved to a new spot.

As I write this, Kevorkian has been released from prison, and is not expected to live much longer. Hepatitis C wrecked him. Time's infernal magic left me deformed and baffled, less ready with quips about the human relics whose ranks I will join soon enough. Jim died in 1989, from non-strawberry-pie-related causes. My mother followed ten years later.

I quit the Stockholm Inn before they found a buyer. I was clever. I would become a wordsmith, and forsake the sweat, grime, and aggravation of menial labor to enter the sublime realm of literature as a famous author. You see how that worked out.

The night after they signed the contracts to unload the Stockholm Inn, my mother pleaded with Jim. She was having second thoughts. Weary as she was of the restaurant grind, she wanted the place back. It was the life they knew.

No, Jim said. Too late.

Free Spatulas
Wendy Spero

The letter was succinct and ominous:

> Dear Recent Graduate:
> Come to our main headquarters on Lexington
> Avenue at 9:00 AM on Monday, June 16th. You will
> get a job.

I had just returned home after college graduation with the desperate hope of finding a job in the city—one that might help me discover what I supposed to be when I grew up. I was too curious not to follow up on this piece of junk mail, so that Monday morning I put on a black and white, sassy yet professional Betsey Johnson dress and, armed with mace, arrived at a "main" office—a large room filled with grey folding chairs and beige rugs covered in questionable stains. There were about thirty of us shuffling about, all roughly the same age and looking equally confused. It was kind of like the movie *Clue*. Everyone was mumbling, "Did you get that *letter*?"

After a significant period of suspense, a young man with far too many blackheads on his forehead made a grand entrance from the bathroom. "Hello! Thank you for coming. You are all probably wondering what this is all about. Well, every single one of you was asked here for the same reason. You were all hard-working students. As of this very moment, you are on the cusp of the greatest money-making opportunity in the history of money-making opportunities." For five minutes he ranted about how life was short and how his cousin almost died at twenty-five and *now*, not later, was the time to improve one's standard of living.

Then, like an afterthought, under his breath, he mumbled that we were really here to interview for a two-month stint selling knives door-to-door. Kitchen knives, for commission.

People started storming out. The guy waved his arms in the air and pleaded, "If you leave now, you are missing out, folks. You'll regret it!" I've never been able to live with regret, so I stayed in my seat eager to see where this was all going and wondering if he'd ever seen a dermatologist for the blackhead problem.

Ten others hesitantly remained with me. Unshaken by the diminished audience, he clumsily wheeled a TV to the front of the room and played a ten-minute-long tape introducing us to the marketing company involved in the venture. There were endless testimonials from a diverse group of young adults. "Knife selling changed everything. It provided marketing experience far more valuable than any expensive business degree." "These knives sell themselves. All I had to do was show up." "Thank goodness I opened that letter and was introduced to the world of knife selling. God knows what kind of degenerate I'd be if I hadn't attended and stayed for the entire duration of that initial meeting."

The guy shut the power off, paused, and frowned. "Now, not everyone can just automatically join our company," he said, tapping one of his blackheads. "We look for *superdooperstars*, not just hard-working students. I'll need to interview you one by one now in the corner area. Wendy Spero, you're first up. Dave Freedman, you're on deck."

I proceeded to the folding chair in the back corner area while the rest of the group watched suspiciously from the other side of the room. He asked me where I had gone to school and what I had studied.

"I went to Wesleya—"

"I think you have something darn special, Wendy. I'd love for you to come aboard. Congratulations! Please stick around for the next portion of the meeting."

I was slightly traumatized by having to look at his blackheads up close but was thrilled to have made the cut. I didn't want to make the others envious, though, so I put on a neutral face and swaggered back to my seat.

One by one, we were all formally accepted into this highly selective marketing conglomerate. Then he sprawled out some knives onto a few chairs facing us, and announced that we'd have to buy an initial knife kit for $100.

As the girl next to me stood up, she whispered, "Get *out!* This is a scam!" But I looked at the shiny cutlery and thought, *I must sell knives*.

Eventually, only two of us were left. The other woman was wearing braces—the clear kind that turn yellow over time. We handed the man credit cards and left with pounds of merchandise and a new purpose in life.

When I immediately informed friends and family that I'd found the perfect summer job, they responded with stilted enthusiasm. I think they worried I had joined a cult and would soon be wearing a flowy skirt and handing out dandelions next to the Holland Tunnel.

The following weekend, Lucy, my best friend from high school, invited me to her family's rented summer house in Martha's Vineyard so I could reboot before officially starting. Because we spent every moment at the beach, and I never motivated to put on sunscreen, I got a *severe* burn on my face. Big red chunks of my skin dangled. I looked like I was in one of those old ABC Afterschool Specials based on a horrible true story, like I'd been burned in a fire by an evil stepmother or something.

Because my face felt so insanely hot, when we smoked weed that Saturday night, it was as though I were experiencing the evening's events from the bong's point of view. I alone could identify with the burning herbs on the receiving end of a pot-head's inhale. It was deep.

When I returned to the city, I rushed to the dermatologist, who could barely hide her fearful reaction to my appearance. She prescribed a soothing white steroid cream for the swelling, and two days later, I grew a spontaneous mustache. A little prickly Fu Manchu one.

So I had the mustache, the burn, and a sack o' knives.

I was ready to sell.

The knife-selling process was a safe, meticulously thought-out scheme. Per the instructions in my knife-selling packet, I called my mom's good, trustworthy friends and politely asked for some names and numbers of their good, trustworthy friends. I then called these people up and performed a well-rehearsed, innocent shtick: "Hi, so, um, so-and-so told me you would be

130

nice enough to help me out. I'm learning about marketing and wondered if I could come over to your house maybe for just a couple minutes and practice selling . . . *things* . . . to you."

Each sucker would reply, "Oh sure, dear, that's sweet. Well, I'm not going to buy anything, but sure—if you want *practice*." Shortly thereafter I'd arrive at their apartment. They'd open the door, notice my deformity and mumble, "Oh. Oh my. Oh dear. Have you tried *aloe*?"

I'd sit at their kitchen table and compliment their hair. We'd gab about our friend in common. Then I'd commence the mind-blowing presentation: I'd slice brown leather into strips with steak knives. I'd cut a thick rope with a bread knife. In one fluid motion, I'd cut a penny in half with large silver sheers. (A thrill in and of itself because cutting currency is technically a federal offense.)

At first my customers would act condescending, politely nodding and mumbling, "Uh huh, yeah, uh huh." But as the presentation progressed, they'd find themselves seeking clarification. "Wait, hold on. How much is that one again?" There was simply no way to remain unaffected by my slick marketing moves.

I was also prepared for the toughest of customer questions. They'd ask, "But wait, if your knives are that sharp, aren't they dangerous?" Unfazed, I'd grin and explain that actually, using one of their *dull* knives was far more risky. "Statistics show that chefs are forty-six percent more likely to slip while cutting a tomato with a worn-down blade."

They'd let out a contemplative, "Huh. Wow. Yeah."

To close the sale I'd lean in, signal for them to lean in, look around (there would only be two of us in the apartment), and whisper, "You know what? I'm not supposed to do this, but I'll give you a free spatula with that bread knife. How's that?" A tiny bit would come out of my commission, but they'd fall for it every time—they'd end up buying an entire set, which they didn't even need in the first place, just to get something for free. Then we'd hug. They'd thank me profusely, and I'd leave with seven hundred of their dollars.

I was thrilled to be good at a real grown-up job, and I didn't feel guilty because at the biweekly knife meetings, the convincing blackhead dude explained over and over again that by selling people these knives, we were massively improving their lives—even if they didn't cook. I was making the world a better place.

I even preyed on our dearest of family friends. My friend Emily recalls her mother telling the family at breakfast that I'd be coming over that afternoon to practice selling "things," and that she might go ahead and buy one item—just to be nice. Later that evening, as the family talked about their days at the dining room table, her father asked, "Oh, so did Wendy come over? Did you end up buying something to be nice?" Emily's mom fell silent. She had spent over $2,000 on knives she didn't remotely need. "Look. Stop hounding me. I don't know what happened!" she moaned. "She . . . she cut leather and then pennies and . . . and I just lost all control. They seemed really necessary at the time . . . I swear . . . We got a free spatula!?"

While I calculated purchase totals and filled out the necessary forms, my clients would happily write down twenty or so names and numbers of friends I could contact. I would call those people up, do the shtick, sell them knives, ask for names, and so on and so on. After three or four weeks I went to so many houses that I had no memory of the original round of victims.

I'd call some random guy and say, "Hi, Mary Bingham recommended that I contact you. She said you might be nice enough to help me out . . . " all the while having no remote idea who Mary was. Then I'd arrive at his door and chat with him for a solid fifteen minutes about Mary's terrific new gig in the Meat Packing District. After noticing the words "cute dog" next to Mary's name on my special knife-selling pad, I'd be sure to add, "And wow, Mary's dog is something, huh?"

Eventually, I started getting calls from people desperately *seeking* knives. "Hello, um, I heard you are a knife expert and you come directly to people's houses . . . can you fit me in? I know you must be so busy. Please. I hear you are the best. I don't trust those pushy salespeople in stores. Salespeople are the worst, ya know?"

Sometimes between appointments I would take a break and wander into a big clothing store like Urban Outfitters. Upon passing through the metal detectors, the entire alarm system would go off. The guard would ask, "Uh, ma'am, what do you have in your bag?" I'd reply, "Knives." He would laugh, and let me in. I was invincible.

The sale of the century occurred one Tuesday afternoon when a friend of a friend of a friend asked me to meet her at her office. As I exited the elevator and walked through the corporate glass double doors, a middle-aged receptionist asked, "Can I help—oh! Are *you* the knife woman?"

"I . . . guess?"

She led me to an enormous conference hall with a stage, got on an intercom and announced, "Attention employees. The knife demonstration will commence in five minutes." *Three hundred* people then poured into the space, and a small fellow with a bowtie got up and bellowed, "With no further ado . . . the floor is *yours*. Do your thang!"

"Heh. All right . . . right . . . OK!" I began. "So, you guys ever cut a tomato and find that the skin gets all mushed?!"

"FUCK YEAH!" yelled the crowd.

Beyond energized, I took out the leather strip and smoothly cut it into thinner strips. I took out the penny and dramatically cut it in half. I took out the impressive bread knife and sliced my left thumb.

Blood was everywhere.

A man shrieked, "Holy—you need to go to the emergency room?"

"Not at all!" I called out nonchalantly. I grabbed a towel from my bag, wrapped it around my hand, held it above my head, applied the necessary pressure, and continued the presentation. And made a fortune.

I was relieved when the summer started to come to an end—my back had begun to ache from schlepping around the heavy mass of metal, and my fingers were covered in Band-Aids. But in order to go out with a bang, a week after my big sale I decided to fly to the annual knife-selling convention in Indianapolis, where I was greeted by large posters of rainbows that read, "Fulfill your potential. Persuade! Sell! Conquer!" At the award ceremony that evening I won a tall trophy *and* a VCR for selling *the most knives* in the Tri-State Area.

The Adolescent Cigarette Salesgirl
And Other Wrong Moves in the Right Direction
Hollis Gillespie

If it were up to me I would have mixed the lemonade with vodka to ensure the product was super popular (probably), but what do I know? Except that it was my daughter's lemonade stand and she has very definite ideas about her own merchandise. "It has to be homemade, with 'real' lemons," she insisted, knowing, even at seven, to make the distinction with me, because she knows I could easily figure out how to make homemade lemonade without using any actual lemons. Don't they sell lemon-flavored chemicals at the store? Put that in a pail, "at home," aim the garden hose at it and—voilà!—homemade lemonade.

But no, Milly meant the kind of lemons that actually grow from the ground, and I guess she is the one to judge because she is the one who had to stand by her product. She's probably right not to listen to me. I have been wrong before—colossally wrong—like once, for three entire months, I thought I had a penis. It didn't help at all that the nurse at the doctor's office confirmed it. "You're having a boy!" she exclaimed, and I, like, *believed* her, until another nurse informed me that my boy sure had a lot of X chromosomes for a boy, which would actually make him a girl, and—*poof!*—there went my penis.

Another time I was wrong was when I thought I'd make a good art salesman, so I got a job at a gallery in the mall. Only it wasn't a real gallery, but one of those places that sell piece-of-shit lithographs signed by filthy rich people like Peter Max and maybe a serigraph here and there of Warhol's "Queen Elizabeth" with real diamond dust brushed on her crown. "Really, it's real," I'd say to customers, incorporating a Vanna White-like hand wave over it, like I was magician's assistant ("Voilà!"). In all I came across as convincing as O.J. professing his innocence. Even so I actually almost got a guy to buy one once, but he was a sweet man with two kids in tow and in the end I didn't have the heart to suck eleven hundred bucks out of his life for something I personally didn't consider worthy of wiping my own ass. I worked there three months and did not sell a thing. Not a single thing. When I look back on that stint, I don't know where I was more wrong: getting the job in the first place or doing it so badly once I had it. But wrong I was. So wrong.

When I was much younger, I tried selling greeting cards door-to-door. I should have known it was a bad idea because my inventory came from a box abandoned by my dad in the garage. Needless to say, my greeting-card venture hit the ground like a safe, probably because the cards were bigger than my third-grade math book and looked like they were made from flammable upholstery.

I thought about this as I watched my girl at her lemonade stand the entire morning and into the afternoon, tending to her little store, which consisted of one sidewalk table under her hand-crafted billboard touting ALL-NATURAL HOMEMADE LEMONADE (COMES WITH COOKIE)!

I was off to the side, as out of sight as I could be without actually being out of sight, which is where I had been relegated because, evidently, beaming with pride is bad for business. Also, all my attempts to flag traffic from the busy street corner in her direction were met with a lukewarm response from the public coupled with consternation from Milly, so I am glad I didn't bother to borrow my friend's gorilla suit in order to bring more attention to myself as I had originally planned.

So instead I simply watched her and marveled at her salesmanship. She didn't even *charge* people. She just had a jar there with a sign on it that read SUGGESTED DONATION: BIG SMILE. That was my idea, which, unlike my other brainstorm—to offer a sugar-free option, which sat there like a pool of rat drool— actually paid off. I had told Milly not to charge an actual price because people are often very generous if you just give them the opportunity.

I know this because I used to sell stuff door-to-door as a kid, which is how my sisters and I spent our afternoons when we weren't playing air hockey at the bar where our father spent his days. The products we sold were the ones he'd abandoned over the years in his many half-hearted attempts to garner an income as we moved from town to town. They would arrive in our home in boxes—which was convenient since we would inevitably be moving again soon, anyway—and that is where they would have stayed if we hadn't nosed around and found them.

We got a lot of rejection as we went door-to-door with these items, but the supply of keychains sold really well thanks to Mr. Festerbeck, our five-hundred-year-old neighbor. He never actually bought anything from us, but he was always a hoot to harass nonetheless. Plus he whistled through his dentures and had so much junk in his front yard it was like picking your way through a rusty bombsite just to make it to his porch. But the most important thing is that the old man always took it upon himself to give us tips on our sales techniques.

"Stand by your product," he'd cackle. "You have to make me think I can't live without it. Like what's this? A keychain? What's so great about this keychain? Looky here, it clips to your belt and it's retractable! Well, my goodness," he'd exclaim, feigning wonderment, "think of the convenience! Think of the ease of use! Think of the bags of groceries that can be saved from being dropped on the front stoop all because this magnificent keychain is at the ready and fumble free! All the cartons of eggs saved from being crushed! This right here will save you time and money! In fact," he gasped, eyes agog, "think of all the pretty ladies who get attacked on their front steps just because they took too long to find their keys in the dark of night! That's how you have to sell it: It can *save your life*."

And off we'd go, laughing, selling our Magnificent Life-Saving Keychains door to door. We got more takers than we would have otherwise thanks to Mr. Festerbeck, who, it turns out, could have used a life-saving device himself. It wasn't long afterward that he was found dead on his kitchen floor by the local exterminator, which explains why he didn't answer his door the last time we knocked. The exterminator had been hired by Mr. Festerbeck's neighbors as a kindly hint to reign in whatever it was that was causing such a terrible bug infestation to emanate from his property, and the exterminator found the problem, all right. But when I think of Mr. Festerbeck I'm careful not to remember that part. Instead I remember his cackle laugh, spry eye, and all that time he spent helping my sisters and me improve our sales technique.

I finally struck a winning streak with the door-to-door gig when, at seven, I started selling homemade cigarettes. It was another idea that had been discarded by my dad, but he discarded all his ideas, not just the bad ones, and you never knew if any of them had actual payoff potential unless you applied a little effort. I remember his cigarette-making machine clearly: It came with a big tin of loose tobacco and little paper sleeves with corresponding filters. And the machine had places you'd put these things and a lever you'd push, and afterward there'd somehow appear an authentic cigarette that, I'm sure, tasted about as good as a burning cat turd.

I pocketed twenty-five cents a pack, so the first day of business I thought I had enough to buy the bongo drum for sale in the window of the liquor store next door to my father's bar. The store's original proprietor was a big man who was fairly scary in appearance with most of the fingers missing from his left hand. My father had once tried to sell him stuff out of the trunk of his car, but the man had informed him plainly, "I'm not buying any of your shit, and I mean that in every possible sense." I myself had been in his store just about every day since we moved into the neighborhood, buying penny candy by the bucket load, and every day that man glared at me, bagged my candy, and scowled as I walked out his door and into the bar next door, where my sisters and I played pool and air hockey to pass the time as my father belted beers and came up with more ideas.

Earlier I'd seen what I thought was a price tag on the bongo drum, for a mere seventy-five cents, showed it to my sisters and everything, but I was wrong. The price tag was actually a rogue sticker on the window right in front of the bongo drum, significant of nothing really, but I thought a price on the window in front of the drum was as good as one on the drum itself and proudly marched to the register one day, slapping two quarters, three nickels, and ten pennies on the counter like I was paying off my parents' mortgage. "What's this?" he said.

"I'm finally buying that drum," I answered, but right then I saw the real price tag. Seven entire dollars! Looking back, I believe that exact moment is the first time I ever felt my heart hit the ground. I thought he was gonna throw me out right then, because once he literally lifted up my eight-year-old neighbor Tom Mulligan by the waistband of his dungarees and tossed him into the crabapple bush across the street, all because Tom peed in the parking lot. So here I was offering that same man seventy-five cents for a $7 drum, and I thought at the very least he'd grab me by my hair and drag me back to the bar to deposit me back on my dad's turf.

"Get outta here," he growled, so I bolted for the door, afraid he was right behind me. But I was wrong. So wrong. "Wait," he yelled after me, and I turned to see him scoop my change into his chopped-up hand. "You forgot your drum." So I was wrong about this guy. But I was remembering him when I told Milly to take donations for her lemonade rather than charging an actual price per cup, and she raked it in. I may be wrong a lot, but I'm right about this: People are often very generous if you just give them the opportunity.

Fine Wines and Liquors
Becky Poole

I had always fancied getting a neighborhood job. I'd lived in Williamsburg for about seven years, long enough to know the folks around the block and feel like part of the community. But I wanted to be more *in* it, to be able to talk to the men who sound like the Godfather, instead of waving while running by to the subway. I wanted an excuse to savor my neighborhood, to see it go on around me, instead of rubbing against the same old neighbors in the bars who drink PBR for fun, wear expensive T-shirts, and do graphic design. Also I was sick of what I had known as the only way to make money for a B.F.A. drama student living in N.Y.C.: working freelance for Viacom. I just couldn't handle all the health benefits. Wink wink. I wanted a job where maybe I could be "the charming girl at the counter," instead of "the weirdo who does comedy and incorrectly sends out our faxes." I already knew the people that worked at the liquor store down the street from my apartment from being a customer and just passing by. Knew them enough to know that they were friendly, all had outside artistic endeavors going on, and had hopes and dreams beyond selling cheap but decent bottles of wine. They were always inviting, creative, willing to listen, give advice, or bend your ear over a taste of wine. It seemed like a good fit to me and, fortunately, to them too. So I figured I'd go for it, forget that the pay was shit, and enjoy the new experience.

Whenever I tell someone new that I work in a liquor store they say, "Isn't that dangerous?" or "Why?" So I'll describe the store's placement in the neighborhood, for a clearer picture of what this store is like. It is located equidistant from the Bottle Shoppe (seller of expensive wines) and your run-of-the-mill Plexiglas, "slide-the-money-over-here" liquor store. And that is pretty much where we are physically and metaphysically. No Plexiglas, but no superiority complex.

In truth, the store feels more like a neighborhood social club for wayward youths than a wine shop. A place for the interesting or eccentric, the harmless ne'er-do-wells and riffraff, to swap naughty stories, share thoughts, poems, and songs.

The obvious perk of working at a wine shop is the free booze, or "tastings" as we like to call them. Wines we haven't tasted before, bottles we seem to have forgotten the taste of, or whatever we feel thirsty for. (For example, "This Jim Beam looks broken, I better just put it in my bag.") Often, a tasting will evolve into an all-night binge with regulars buying bottles that we open there to taste more of. Then we all chatter, cackle, and stumble down to the local Irish bar, or hipster bar, whichever one has somewhere to sit or isn't having a goddamn karaoke night. And if we're lucky someone's having a rooftop party or backyard BBQ. Our crew may be late but we always come with booze.

At any job you are immediately thrown into a new social circle: brand new friends, brand new comfort zones, brand new make-outs. With this job it was like immediately being thrown into a barrel of drunken monkeys. As suspected, my drinking spiked about the same time that I started working. I was a kid in a candy store. Valpolicella? Sangiovese? Never heard of it, and I certainly should be able to discuss it with the customers. *Glug, glug, glug.* Into the plastic dollar store cup it goes. I'm learning.

As for my co-workers, there are only four of us at the moment. Randy the gregarious singer-songwriter, music man in a fedora, who always wears black and can spin a great yarn. Everyone knows Randy and everyone loves Randy. Anthony the manager, he's the neighborhood guy. Grew up on the same street as the shop and worked there when it used to be the best damn pizza in the neighborhood. Bretney: she's young, hip, hot, and witty. She has her own line of hand-sewn handbags that we sell in the back. There was a guy who worked there right as I started whom I need to mention. Tall, bespectacled Chris, the crazy poet/musician who wore shirts with his face looking back up at him and sometimes talked in just noises. He moved to Kentucky with his lady friend.to have a baby. (It's *ador*able.)

And then there are the regulars, customers who turn into good acquaintances and extended friends. The people who I never might have met that live right next to me. People like Lynn, a woman in her early sixties, a sort of hippie/new age massage therapist who throws parties, helps us plan our spiritual lives (whether we want to or not), and parties like a rock star. She's like the mother hen who always smells like lavender and blacks out sometimes. Don, a previous employee who is fabulous, life of the party, loud, and as full of great ideas as his iPod is full of Madonna songs. Benanna (like Bennifer or TomKat) is a couple so wrong for each other it's right. She's a lawyer; he's a troublemaker with a heart of gold and a cast-iron liver. Then there is the adorable couple so right for each other it's right; when they walk down the street you can imagine them thirty years later happily doing the same thing. He's a soft-spoken chef; she's a poet, teacher, and confidant. The Beam Boys, three happy guys in Brooklyn from the Dominican Republic who come over from the OTB and get a half-pint of Jim Beam three to four times a night. When asked why they don't just get a fifth, they say they don't want to get too drunk (but we know, it's harder to hide a fifth). There's also the Williamsburg fencing team; as far as I can tell they just get loaded and go to naked parties together, I've never seen any gear. Vince, a retired model that never talks about it and would rather show us his latest yoga poses and talk about how awesome the library is; he's so sweet it's almost creepy. Gustav, the compulsive bipolar technophile who likes LEDs, making bikes, and occasionally dressing up like a bunny rabbit. And let's not forget the guy who lives in the back (just until he can find a place). But hey, he's cute, and he works there now. I guess it was like a welfare-to-work deal. Oh, and all the crushes. My my my, so many indy boys, so little time. It is oddly satisfying to watch people's lives change as they stop in. Being happy and sad for them because you know part of their story. Which is also sort of sad, because you're still just the girl who works at the liquor store to lots of them probably. Sniff.

One of the first nights I remember hanging out after work, we all (the employees and regulars entourage) went out together to a party. This night is now referred to as Fight Night. We headed jovially out one Saturday night to a rooftop party of Don's. As the party morphed into drunken globs of people goo, a roommate got handsy with Anna (of Benanna) and said sleazy things to yours truly. Ben (of Benanna) is prone to fisticuffs and face-planting drunkenness. At this point in the evening, he was close to both. There was no stopping this train. All of a sudden there were grown men rolling around on a couch awkwardly punching and even scratching each other (the other guy of course!). This may have been the moment I fell in love with my new job. I was so happy! I had a crew who would fight for me! Finally, my Brooklyn crew!

Of course there are sides to the job that are pretty depressing. I mean, if an alcoholic needs a fix they're coming to where I work. It's hard to see someone come in and know that this is really not the place they should be. Who am I to judge? Really, when do you have to say no? I always thought it'd be clear, and I have the right, *blah blah blah*. Well, you try being four-foot-eleven and telling a drunken six-foot-five man who speaks only Polish and is not taking no for an answer, "no." That "no" quickly becomes, "$4.97 please."

It's hard for a Minnesotan like myself to lose the happy chattiness even after ten years in N.Y.C. I am what I am, a friendly, flirty gal. But I can be taught new tricks. A lesson I learned early: Freaks should not be flirted with. It's a good tip to learn for any retail job really. But *sometimes* it just happens. The brooding, mumbling poet only seems shy. And the next morning has killed a kitten and placed it ever so gently on your stoop. Its tiny paws posed as if to say, "Hold me!" Maybe later that week Jack Kero-wacko shows up at your place of work inebriated, just to talk. Eventually following you to a party. At the end of the night you try to be nice and joke off the end-of-the-night-kiss moment—It came out of nowhere! You never invited or intended on having it!—with a, "Ha-ha, awkward! Well, see you later!" Only to hear (and quite clearly at that, Mr. Mumbly!) a word of wisdom from the modern day beatnik as he turns and swerves down a Brooklyn side street: "Bitch!" Oh god, great. I fumble with the keys, thinking maybe he won't remember the house number, or the three giant angels that the Italian landlords have placed oh-so-ostentatiously on the front gate . . . I mean, they're unremarkable really, right? . . . *crap!* But I severely digress.

Sometimes working there feels like a kind of purgatory. We can't leave and some people like to stay. I like to think the job has all the perks of bartending, with none of the tips! Like a bartender we hear stories of woe, stories of triumph, and just some stories. Unlike a bartender, there is normally no one else around to distract us from the conversation intermittently. Until a story gets really good, then without fail someone comes in and asks for your finest white zinfandel.

But it isn't all bad; sitting out on the railing of the handicap entrance ramp in front of the store (the pizza place installed it before they moved out), you start to feel like you're surveying the land. Peeking out of a saloon watching the hipsters, crazy people, and Italian lifers scurry, grumble, and waddle respectively by. They are smiling and waving at neighbors on their way to a productive day or night on the town. Youngsters swear at and punch each other lovingly. Lovers saunter past distractedly. By and by, lots of couples buy wine. Lots of attractive, seemingly happy couples in the prime of their lives just love a pinot noir. The store atmosphere is ripe for encounters, if not romance. What with all the wine tasting, and hot new hipsters moving in, all cocky and stupid. *Mmmm*, delicious twenty-three-year-olds, they pass by and I feel like a Southern woman of leisure out on her veranda licking the edge of a mint julep and fanning away the vapors. But the real picture is my drinking cheap red wine out of a plastic cup, staring uncomfortably, and laughing too loudly. Like ya do.

Randy said something once to the effect of, "We have a tendency to look at different times in our life as being incongruous." Like time capsules that we look at as having nothing to do with each other. But they all collide somewhere. I feel like I needed this job to mean something. And as I plan my move out of New York City after these ten years, I think, even though I make less than $10 an hour, I wouldn't trade this experience for anything. I learned more about my neighborhood in working there for one year, than living there for seven. Running in and out of my apartment, racing to a packed subway, to a crappy temp job, to an audition, to a show, to spend more money. I never stopped to take a sniff, if you will. It was really nice to sit on the stoop, have some wine, talk smart, and watch the people pass through my neighborhood. The store is a people aquarium, a broken heart hospital, a dance club, a rehearsal space, a community center for downtrodden (not so) youths, and I got to be a part of that. Overall, I liked everyone that came in, I *liked* my job. Now I find myself leaving the neighborhood I've called home for eight years and I feel like I really lived there. It is a part of me and I was a part of it.

Cheers!

The Bad Call
Clay Allen

There were a million reasons to take the job at Sexworld. It was ironic and irony is valued in our society, it was a rite of passage for an overeducated kid from the suburbs, and Sexworld gave employees a solid discount. The universe was calling me to go and see some fucked-up shit, and I heard that call loud and clear.

Two days after I graduated college, my meal plan gone forever, I found myself driving to Minneapolis and moving in with a hermetic friend who attended art school there. I found clean, shiny Minneapolis strange and lonely. I bought a cheap bike and took long rides, trying to figure out what I was supposed to be doing.

My first thought was that I might try to break into the ad game. It seemed a good fit for someone with no tangible skills. I wrote some specs and called in a few connections, but I gave up quickly when I didn't receive a hero's welcome. I hadn't learned much in film school, few people do, but the one thing they taught me was that if the value of fresh, uncorrupted talent wasn't immediately recognized and richly rewarded, then fuck them in the ass with a hat rack.

In reality, I had no idea how to get a real job. The only advice my dad gave me was to dress up like a pizza man and take pizzas to people I wanted to meet with. I fancied myself a risk-taker, but I couldn't bring myself to do it.

So I rode around until I found exactly what I knew I shouldn't be looking for.

Sexworld. A two-story smut emporium spread out in an enormous converted warehouse. The main floor housed the bulk of the porn, divided into sections by genre and then again by studio. There were magazines from every corner of the world, and more than a few local publications, which I thought was generous. There was even a smoke shop, which sold cigarettes, bongs, whippets, and balloons.

And then there was the next-level stuff. Live-girl booths, complete with a leather-bound menu of shows. Video booths were upstairs, sixty of them, along with the queer porn, S&M gear, and hooker clothes. This was all tied together by a friendly (but creepy) circus theme. When I saw a restraining apparatus selling for $6,800, I conceded that Sexworld was truly deserving of its name.

The interview process took all of fifteen minutes, the most complicated part being the photocopying of my driver's license. As Tory, my twenty-six-year-old, neck-tattooed boss fumbled with the machine, I watched a pair of lesbians dildo shopping on the security monitors. "God bless them and their vaginas," I thought proudly, "God bless us all."

Tory kicked the photocopier, oblivious. "Wear whatever you want, don't take shit from anybody, and don't steal anything," he muttered through drags of a Pall Mall. Maybe I would get to be like that, unfazed by people shopping for things to have sex with. But it would never happen. I too-greatly enjoyed the contortions of thrill, desire, and shame.

For my first day of work, per Tory's instructions, I wore white pants, green shoes, and a sleeveless T-shirt depicting Shaquille O'Neal as Shazam. A checkered golf cap completed my *ensemble*.

"You look like the ice cream man," Tory told me when I showed up. I was fairly sure that was a compliment.

They let me cut my teeth in the smoke shop, and then I was posted in the Triangle, the oozy-cruzy upstairs section, where people into "other stuff" shopped. My hours would be 12 to 9 AM.

I was asked to stay up through paper-thin hours of the night selling the dirtiest porn to the sketchiest people in an unfamiliar city. This was asked of me by a man who considered his body lice a political statement. I didn't argue. It was the call, and I had to follow it. I dressed stupid, drank rivers of coffee, and smoked a hole into my left lung.

It was a savage turn, but having made it, I was given front-row seats to the show. I watched a drunk Native American stumble out of the bathroom covered in vomit and he tried to sucker-punch Dennis, the 250-pound clerk who worked overnights with me. Dennis, incidentally, was the driver of the Sexworld car in the Jordan County demolition derby. This was a tough dude, a for-*real* dude. It only took him one shot to take the drunk down, followed by several kicks of a steel-toed boot that served as the man's escort out of Sexworld into what would otherwise be a perfect Midwestern summer dawn.

I sold lube and poppers to an endless stream of cruisers, their eyes furtive and guilty, their hearts practically leaping through their throats.

I engaged in a heated argument with a hooker who tried the old "price-tag switcheroo" on a pair of red leather boots. I argued with logic, she called me the *N*-word, in earnest, which hurt much worse than I'd expected.

I watched on the security monitors as men would come out of the video booths after masturbating and stick their hands straight into the "serve yourself" popcorn maker we kept by the elevator. There was a scoop available, of course, but I guess some folks just wanted a handful.

Overnight hours melted much-needed body weight from my bones and turned my head into pea soup. Though still somehow amusing, it became hard to remember what the point of this had been.

And then I saw what was clearly the most fucked-up shit you could ever want to see in a porno store. I knew it the second the elevator doors opened. This is it, I thought. This is why I've been called here.

It was between one and two in the morning. The coffee was still fresh and I was on my first cigarette of the night. Bar-time folks were having their fun, sales were breezy, when my radio went off.

"Yo, bro." It was Dennis. "Watch this group coming up."

The elevator doors opened and out they came: seven retarded adults guided by a shiny young couple in matching visors.

A sight such as this begs a series of urgent questions, which you may be asking yourselves now: Who's charged these two children with the care of seven mentally challenged adults at this no-good hour of the night? And being that they look like they've never made it past second base themselves, how did they agree on Sexworld as the outing's destination?

Even if you could reasonably answer those two questions, is

there any possible explanation for herding these people onto a sticky elevator and taking them up to the most perverted section of Sexworld, where herpes is transmitted by sight?

There were no answers. Not for me. There was only abject horror as I watched, mouth agape, as retarded people fingered boxes like *Big Bear, Little Bear* and *Granny Fucks A Tranny!!!* They swerved in and out of the booths, pushing buttons, playing with the doors. Cruisers vanished, forsaking free popcorn for a speedy exit. Overweight retarded men and women walked through the aisles holding hands, clapping, laughing, cheering for the dildos, the group leaders right there with them.

A man in a dingy yellow shirt ran up to the counter and dug his hands into a bowl of lube singles.

"Candy!" he screamed.

"No, not candy," college visor said, smiling at me. It was the kind of smile that said, "Thanks for your patience, I know it's strange, but I'm a better person than you because I'm helping and you work at Sexworld." They used the Triangle like a playground for about twenty minutes and left without buying anything.

I cried when I rode my bike home that morning. In white tennis shorts and a child-sized cardigan sweater, coming from my overnight shift at the porno superstore, I knew that to the nine-to-fivers I was an equally sad spectacle to what I'd witnessed earlier that night.

As the summer drew to a close, I quit quietly and made arrangements to move back to New York. Tory saw it coming. "Guys like you don't last very long," he told me. Thank Christ. When I got to my folks' place in Chicago, I slept for a hundred years. When I woke up, the call that had seemed so important and real was now remarkably distant, like the sound of a kickball bounced on a deserted playground blacktop. Today, if I listen hard and pretend I never needed forgiveness, I can just hear it.

The Popsicle Shop
Jane Borden

Although the Popsicle Shop was technically a children's clothing store, kids were rarely there. They don't like having frilly jumpers yanked on and off their heads so they can be paraded around the room in front of women who play bridge with their mothers. They pitch fits. Or at least I did. So my mom usually went alone, returning with several outfits for me to try on where no one could hear the screams. She didn't have to pay for any of it. The store gave her everything "on approval," trusting that she'd return what didn't fit—or what hadn't been stained or ripped in the process, at which point, my father was mailed the bill.

The mothers in our wealthy North Carolina neighborhood rewarded such convenience with fierce loyalty. No one dreamed of shopping anywhere else, regardless of the store's high prices and thin selection. And, anyway, they were all friends with the owners, whose children went to school with their children, whose Christmas-card photos were displayed in the picture frames for sale in the store. You know that village? The one it takes to raise a child? That's the Popsicle Shop—so much so that once I outgrew the stock, I moved behind the counter. I started my very first job at fourteen, below the legal age of employment. *Enh*, our village had its own rules.

Once on the other side, I learned that leaving kids at home was more than just something that happened (everyone had full-time "housekeepers" babysitting at home) but that the phenomenon, in turn, was good for business. Untouched by the realities of childhood, the Popsicle Shop was a fantasyland. Customers' homes were filled with snot, dirt, and tiny people who peed on the floor. Not so at the Popsicle Shop, where the air was scream-free, scabby Band-Aids were never stuck into the carpet, and no one had cheese underneath her fingernails. It's what every woman dreams having children will be like: precious, pristine, and pastel. Like little Stepford babies. We sold this illusion. Women waded through rows of eyelet-trimmed dresses and lacy short-suits ("oh, yes ma'am, those *are* for boys") in ecstatic wonder. To the pregnant, excited by potential energy, it was porn. To aging mothers, holding on to the past, it was crack.

Since my older sisters had also worked there, it was decided before I even had a checking account that I would too. There was no application to fill out. And I didn't need a resume. I did, however, wear a Popsicle Shop dress to the interview . . . because it was conducted at a neighborhood cocktail party.

"So are you ready to come work for us now?"

"Yes ma'am."

"How about this Saturday?"

My time there was less of a job than a rite of passage. Although a freshman in high school, I was still a child—in the way that all high school freshmen are still children. My mother had to drop me off and pick me up. I'd never been kissed. I wore braces. And I was growing out a wickedly heinous perm. In short, it was the perfect time for me to be sent away from society on an adolescent journey. Perhaps to travel through Latin America painting churches, or to spend a summer with an estranged uncle in Maine, or to live in the woods waiting for menstruation.

Instead, during my awkward period, I was thrust into society's spotlight. The store was basically an extension of our country club and the majority of employees were impeccably coiffed ladies from the neighborhood: my mother's friends and my friends' mothers. Anything and everything could be reported home. Some of my fellow employees treated me, with reason, like the child I was. Mrs. Donald, for example, pumped me for information, looking for grist to fuel what my friends and I called "the grocery-store gossip"—the circuit through which moms traded information about each other's children. Get caught sneaking out of your own home and your parents will keep the incident quiet. Get caught sneaking out of someone else's home and your name will be whispered among cantaloupe-thumping ladies at the Harris Teeter.

Mrs. Baker, on the other hand—and she insisted I call her Susan—would gossip *with* me. It was tame, mind you; I never heard about affairs, divorces or—*shhh*—alcoholism! Still, it exemplified trust. Her aim was to treat me like an adult, or, to be more specific, a Southern lady. It was while working with Susan that I had a realization. It was while stocking embroidered footies that I figured out something major: I was being groomed. Southern women don't get to go live in the woods; we're moved directly into the drawing room to help with the knitting.

Of course, we didn't actually knit—that would happen later, when it became ironically hip. These were modern, liberated women who left home to work and got paid for it. It's just that their jobs were still in the child-rearing arena. I was drenched in motherhood. Everywhere I looked, I had glimpses of where I might be in my future. In ten years: shopping for my own children while wearing oversized jeans, a ponytail, and driving a minivan. In thirty years: dressed in a wool pantsuit, drenched in a terrific display of jeweled baubles, and requesting extra ribbon on the gift I bought for my neighbor's new baby. Or—in the case of the elderly, slightly demented Mrs. Halloway—in sixty years: buzzing through the store in a zip-up robe and slippers, while my Cadillac runs in the parking lot. Every high society has its Edith Bouvier Beale.

Working at the Popsicle Shop was a job acceptable for a lady. Still, most employees took it on as a hobby. These were not times of war; we were not Rosie the Riveters. (In fact, if Rosie had ever come in, she wouldn't have been given anything "on approval," which naturally required being approved of.) Furthermore, I was not the only one for whom this was a first job. In her fifties, Mrs. Stacker had finally entered the workforce. She'd had a full life of committees, clubs, and card games, sure; she'd just never received a paycheck for any of it. I assume she'd never managed a checkbook or paid a bill either, because she couldn't grasp the concept of a sale. Although we did have one computer, it was kept in the back and used only by the owners. Everything in the front of the store was handwritten on carbon-copied paper bills. If one wanted to pay by Visa, we were to make a carbon copy of the card in one of those plastic swiping machines and then punch the code into a small, wired keypad in order to transfer the funds.

A couple of months after Mrs. Stacker started working

shifts, book discrepancies popped up, and several local ladies called to explain that their cards had not been charged. Upon investigation, the owners found a stack of carbon slips in a drawer near the cash register. Mrs. Stacker had simply been swiping the cards, and then putting the pieces of paper in a drawer, where they still sat, looking very dainty and organized.

I imagine, at some point in her life, someone told Mrs. Stacker not to worry, that she'd never have to know how to work a cash register or manage a checkbook. I imagine this because a similar thing was told to me. While home from college one spring weekend, I sat at the kitchen table finishing dinner while my father worked on our taxes.

"You know what, Dad? I should really know how to do this. I'm an adult now; I should take care of my own taxes. If you show me now, I'll do it myself from here on out."

At that point, my mother spun around—she was doing dishes, literally wearing an apron and yellow rubber gloves—and said, in her beautiful, singsong Virginian lilt, "Sweetheart, you will *never* have to do your own taxes." This is the Southern dichotomy: that my mother could take part in such a scene, when she herself is an entrepreneur, a small-business owner, and a successful one at that.

There are simply some things a lady does not do. According to my grandmother, one of those things was cleaning houses. I took a job babysitting to make extra cash in college. Acceptable. After hearing the mother complain about the ineptitude and expense of Molly Maids, a local cleaning service, I offered to do a more thorough job for less money. I was rolling in dough until I made the mistake of offhandedly mentioning my entrepreneurial venture to my grandmother. A granddaughter of hers?

Performing such a menial task? She was despondent. She wouldn't stand for it. She offered to pay me $100 a month *not* to do it. And she did—every month until she died.

"Do you promise you're not cleaning houses?"

"Yes ma'am."

"Here you go."

Even though I mostly didn't work in college, I at least knew how. At fourteen, however, I *was* incompetence. I may have been a good student, but employment eluded me—especially at the Popsicle Shop because I knew nothing about the ins and outs of having children.

"My son is two but only weighs twenty-four pounds—do you think I should go a size smaller in this jumper?"

"Um . . . the capital of New York is Albany?"

Eventually, customers deduced I was useless. They'd ask straightaway for one of the owners or manager, and if none was in, respond, "I'll come back tomorrow!" Mostly I ran the register—being good at math—and answered the phone.

"Hello, Popsicle Shop!"

"What flavors you got?"

"Uh, we don't actually sell popsicles."

"My bad!"

This happened far too often for them to have all been pranks. And I empathized with the confusion: I worked there and still didn't get it. I was surrounded by lacy underpants, crocheted bonnets, and pink plush bears, yet I was expected to act like an adult. I was too old for the clothes, but too young for the responsibility.

This psychological confusion had a physical manifestation: the preteen rack. In a misguided effort to stunt growth, some

160

mothers made their children shop at the Popsicle Shop well beyond the proper age. The rack was the tangible equivalent of putting a brick on their heads. Basically, the preteen rack housed larger versions of the same styles otherwise available, along with a few forward-thinking, adult ensembles—like, cats were still smocked on a dress, but their fur was rendered in primary colors instead of pinks. Although the small rack had a few dedicated customers, it made everyone else uncomfortable. People don't want hints of adulthood contaminating their Stepford baby illusion. In other words, some of the garments had darts in the chest area. And tiny breasts are *not* adorable.

The act of working there also put a brick on my head. When the store was empty, I actually played with the toys that we kept in the dressing rooms. I rubbed my hands all over the couture stuffed animals. I even, from time to time, made purchases: a small hand-painted lamp, a miniature pillow with eyelet trim, a tiny lace hairclip. You know the ones that are just ribbons and Velcro? That clasp onto the only three wisps of hair a two-month-old has? Right. I wore it over my ear. Just to round out the visual, on any given school day I might have also been wearing the snake-and-eyeball ring I'd saved up $80 to purchase from the hippie store downtown called Light Years. Like any teenager, I was the hodgepodge product of several competing influences. I was confused.

While my health teacher tried to deter us from teen pregnancy, I spent Saturdays thinking about which outfits I'd dress *my* children in. And to be sure, working at the Popsicle Shop made you want kids. At the same time, I'd done enough babysitting to know that the Stepford baby thing was truly an illusion. Sure, picking out itty-bitty outfits for the window display was my favorite part of the job, but it was because I liked playing with dolls, not because I wanted one.

In my sophomore year, I went away to boarding school and stopped working at the Popsicle Shop. Then there was college. And, now, New York, where I finally found those woods I wanted to escape into, far away from the village of beautiful women who raised me. They cleared one path so that I could forge another. I still keep that tiny pillow on my bed. The hand-painted lamp sits on the coffee table by my apartment door. And, every now and then, I wear the clip over my ear. In other words, I may have a grown-up job, pay my own rent, and bank online, but I still don't do my taxes.

Sixteen Retail Rules
Catie Lazarus

1. True or false:

    a) As a shopper, you should know the difference between "dressy casual" and "shabby chic."

    b) Couture clothing shouldn't be functional.

    c) Babies need headbands, sweater vests, and jewelry as much as grown-ups do.

2. If you lost your parent, ask the security guard to broadcast across the mall's PA system, "Jesus Christo, please report to the shoe department."

3. People love to hear you discipline your children, so let the kids have a temper tantrum until they tire themselves out.

4. The correct term for someone who works in retail is:

    a) Salesperson.

    b) Sales assistant.

    c) Sales associate.

    d) Salesclerk.

    e) Sales staff.

    f) Sales personnel.

    g) Slave.

5. You'll lose enough weight to warrant buying tight jeans.

6. When your deodorant stains a silk shirt you're trying on, distract the salesperson by complaining that "silk is so last season."

7. Feeling unsure about how an expensive item looks, demand that the sales associate who makes money on commission give you an honest opinion.

8. If the clothing doesn't look good on the dummy sized 36-18-22, it'll probably look smart on you.

9. When a sales assistant is helping someone else:

   a) Cut in, as you are in more of a hurry. Also, venting helps.

   b) Offer your unsolicited opinion, especially if it's negative.

   c) Hover until your eyes bleed from staring.

10. Scratch and peel scaly feet when trying on shoes, especially if you have a case of athlete's foot.

11. When trying on a bathing suit, remove your undergarments so other customers can get to know you intimately, without even knowing your name.

12. When swapping a cheaper price tag for the actual legitimate one, remind yourself that "the man" deserves this! (Also, don't ask the salesclerk if pay will be deducted or job called into question.)

13. Speak on your cell phone while in line for the cashier only if you are:

   a) Cooing in baby talk to your doggy-woggy.

   b) Having a phone therapy session, be it as patient or doctor.

   c) Fighting with your ex-husband about palimony.

   d) All of the above.

14. The more emotionally dramatic and loud you complain, the more effective, particularly when returning a used item without a receipt.

15. After forgetting to get your parking ticket validated at the mall, just assume the parking attendant will empathize about how your shopping trip was stressful.

16. True or false:

    a) Salespeople prefer to hang the items themselves, so leave them in a ball on the floor.

    b) "It's a steal" means the item is yours for free, to have and to hold, till death do you part.

ABOUT THE AUTHORS

JEFF MARTIN is a writer from Tulsa, Oklahoma. He regularly contributes commentaries to public radio and writes about books for several publications. He has worked in retail for quite some time, and depending on the success of this book, may be doing so for quite some time.

NEAL POLLACK is the author of several acclaimed books of satirical fiction, including *The Neal Pollack Anthology of American Literature* and the novel *Never Mind the Pollacks*. He recently turned his attention to nonfiction with the publication of *Alternadad*, a book on early parenthood. He lives in Los Angeles, California with his family.

WADE ROUSE is the author of the critically acclaimed *America's Boy: A Memoir* and has worked in public relations for some of the nation's most prestigious private schools, colleges, and universities. His latest book is *Lattes & Land Rovers: The Confessions of a Prep School Mommy Handler*. He lives in Michigan. www.waderouse.com

STEWART LEWIS is the author of the novel *Rockstarlet* and his most recent release is the novel *Relative Stranger*. He is a native of Boston, now living in New York City. www.stewartlewis.com

ELAINE VIETS is the author of the *Dead-End Job* mystery series and numerous short stories. An Anthony and Agatha Award winner, she lives in Fort Lauderdale, Florida, with her husband. www.elaineviets.com

JIM DEROGATIS is the pop music critic for the *Chicago Sun-Times* and host of *Sound Opinions* on Chicago Public Radio. He is the author of several books. www.jimdero.com

KEVIN SMOKLER's writing has appeared in the *San Francisco Chronicle, The Believer, ReadyMade,* and on National Public Radio. He lectures nationwide about the future of reading, writing, and publishing, and is the director of the Virtual Book Tour. His most recent book is *Bookmark Now.* He lives in San Francisco, California. www.kevinsmokler.com

MICHAEL BEAUMIER is a frequent contributor to NPR's *This American Life* and the author of *I Know You're Out There*, a humorous and touching book about what it's like to work in the personals department of an alternative weekly newspaper.

ANITA LIBERTY is the author of the books *How To Heal the Hurt by Hating, How to Stay Bitter through the Happiest Times of Your Life*, and most recently, *The Center of the Universe (Yep, That Would Be Me).* www.anitaliberty.com

RICHARD COX is the author of *Rift* and *The God Particle.* www.richardcox.net

JAMES WAGNER is the author of *The False Sun Recordings*. His work has appeared in *The American Poetry Review, Denver*

Quarterly, McSweeney's, and elsewhere. He lives in Syracuse, New York.

VICTOR GISCHLER is the author of 4 hard-boiled crime novels, including the Edgar Award-nominated *Gun Monkeys*. His most recent book is *Go-Go Girls of the Apocalypse*. He lives with his wife and family in Baton Rouge, Louisiana. www.victorgischler.blogspot.com

C.A. CONRAD is the author of *Deviant Propulsion*. He co-edits *FREQUENCY* audio journal, and edits the 9for9 project. He lives and writes in Philadelphia. www.caconrad.blogspot.com

GARY MEX GLAZNER is the author of *How to Make a Living as a Poet* and *How to Make a Life as a Poet*. Glazner's group the Precision Poetry Drill Team was featured on NPR's *All Things Considered*. Glazner is the Managing Director of the Bowery Poetry Club in New York City. He and his wife live outside of Santa Fe, New Mexico. www.howtopoet.blogspot.com

TIMOTHY BRACY was a founding member of the New York City-based rock band The Mendoza Line. Their final album, released in 2007, was *30 Year Low*.

COLSON WHITEHEAD was born and raised in New York City. His first novel, *The Intuitionist* was a finalist for the PEN/Hemingway. His next work, *John Henry Days*, was a *New York Times* Editor's Choice, won the Young Lions Award and was a finalist for the National Book Critics Circle and the Pulitzer Prize. *The Colossus of New York* was a *New York Times* Notable Book of a Year. Whitehead has also been the recipient of a

Whiting Writer's Award and a MacArthur Grant. His writing has appeared in the the *New York Times*, the *Village Voice*, *Salon*, and *Newsday*. His most recent novel is *Apex Hides the Hurt*. He lives in Brooklyn, New York with his wife Natasha and daughter Madeline. www.colsonwhitehead.com

RANDALL OSBORNE He has worked as an editor/writer for more newspapers than he likes to think about. His writing has appeared in the *Atlanta Journal-Constitution*, the *St. Louis Dispatch*, the *Progressive*, and various others, including www.salon.com and www.playboy.com. He lives in the San Francisco Bay Area.

WENDY SPERO is and award-winning comedian and actress. She has performed on NPR, Comedy Central, VH1, and NBC. Her latest book is *Microthrills: True Stories from a Life of Small Highs*. www.wendyspero.com

HOLLIS GILLESPIE is a *Writer's Digest* Breakout Author of the Year and a regular commentator on NPR's *All Things Considered*. She is the author of *Confessions of a Recovering Slut and Other Love Stories* and *Bleachy-Haired Honkey Bitch*, which *Vanity Fair* called "rib-crackingly funny." She lives in Atlanta, Georgia. www.hollisgillespie.com

BECKY POOLE is a comedian living in New York City. She co-hosts a monthly show called *HERsterical* with her comedy duo partner, Noelle Romano, and performs with the sketch comedy group MEAT. www.funnymeat.com

CLAY ALLEN is a writer and performer. He lives in Los Angeles, California.

JANE BORDEN is a writer and comedy editor for *Time Out New York*.

CATIE LAZARUS is a comedian and writer. Emerging Comics of New York awarded her the Best Comedy Writer and the *New York Resident* selected her as a Top 100 New Yorker for comedy.

ACKNOWLEDGEMENTS

First off, attention must be paid to all of the fine people at Counterpoint/Soft Skull for all of their time, advice, encouragement, and hard work. The top of that list is reserved for the intrepid Richard Nash, without whom this project would have never left the ground.

The following is a list (in no specific order) of various people I would like to thank for various things: Catie Lazarus, David Rakoff, Richard Cox, Owen King, all of my pals at the Tulsa City-County Library (especially the women of the Schusterman-Benson), my retail coworkers (past and present), Teresa Miller, everyone at Public Radio Tulsa (KWGS), the entire crew at OETA, Patricia Marx, Wayne & Nancy Harrison, Will & Julie Thomas, and Bettina Dirks.

I would also like to thank all of my friends and family, especially my parents. Without you I never would have been able to make my childhood dream of working in retail come true. Just kidding. I love you.

Last but not least, Molly. If not for retail, I never would have found you. And for that, I will always be grateful.